Revive and Thrive:

The Art of Town Revitalization and Historical Preservation

HARLAN G. OTIS

OTIS
PUBLISHING

First edition

This book was professionally typeset on Reedsy.
Find out more at reedsy.com

Contents

Introduction

Welcome to this educational and transformative journey into Town and Historic Revitalization. This book is more than just another treatise on the theoretical aspects of architecture and urban renewal. Instead, it stands as a bridge between our towns' rich historical fabric and the practical, actionable strategies that can breathe new life into them. Our exploration is rooted in the belief that revitalization is both an art and a science, requiring a deep appreciation of our past as well as innovative approaches to future challenges.

At the heart of this book lies a unique approach that intertwines the architectural significance of historic towns with straight-forward, step-by-step revitalization strategies. This dual focus ensures that as we chart a course toward rejuvenating our communities, we also pay homage to the architectural heritage that gives each town its unique character.

Structured to serve as your comprehensive guide, the book unfolds in carefully crafted chapters. Each section builds on the last, starting with an overview of the principles of town and historic revitalization, moving through the importance of community involvement, and culminating in a collection of practical strategies designed for real-world application. Along the way, we will dive into case studies, engage with exercises that put theory into practice and offer specific recommendations that you can adapt to your local context.

Community involvement is the cornerstone of any successful revitalization effort. True transformation can occur through the collective energy, insights, and dedication of local residents, business owners, and stakeholders. This book emphasizes the power of community-led initiatives, offering guidance on how to galvanize support, foster collaboration, and create a shared vision for your town's future.

To you, the reader, whether you are an enthusiast of archi-tecture, a professional looking to make a tangible impact, or simply someone who cares deeply about the future of your community, this book is for you. My hope is that it serves not only as a source of inspiration but also as a practical toolkit that empowers you to take action.

As we stand on the brink of this revitalization journey, I invite you to join me. Together, let us redefine the landscapes of our towns, preserving their history while paving the way for a vibrant, sustainable future. The path ahead is filled with potential; let's embark on this transformative journey together.

Let the revitalization begin.

Chapter 1: The Foundations of Revitalization

The potential for remarkable transformations lies in the quiet corners of bustling cities and the forgotten outskirts of small towns. These places, steeped in history yet often overlooked, are the canvases for the art and strategy of town and historic revitalization. This chapter serves as the cornerstone of understanding what revitalization entails— not merely a facelift but a deep, respectful rejuvenation of cultural and architectural heritage. As you delve into this exploration, consider a town you know, perhaps one you call home. How has it changed? What stories do the old walls and pavements hold? It's within these reflections that the essence of revitalization begins to stir, promising not just economic uplift but a rekindling of community spirit and historical pride.

1.1 Defining Town and Historic Revitalization: Goals and Benefits

Understanding Revitalization

Revitalization is a term often tossed around in community meetings and architectural reviews, yet its depth is sometimes lost in translation. It transcends the basic concept of renovation, which implies mere repair and restoration, aiming instead to reinvigorate and infuse new life into spaces that form the crux of our communal and historical identity. Historic revitalization respects the past's architecture and stories, integrating them with modern needs to foster places that are not only aesthetically pleasing but vibrant and economically robust. This holistic approach ensures that revitalization is not an act of preservation in isolation but a forward-looking strategy that prepares towns for future generations while celebrating their historical narratives.

Setting Goals

The primary objectives of revitalization projects can be as diverse as the communities they serve. However, core goals resonate across different towns and cities: preserving historical significance, enhancing community appeal, and stimulating economic growth. Preserving historical significance involves safeguarding architectural styles, important landmarks, and artifacts that collectively narrate the town's heritage. Enhancing community appeal focuses on creating inviting public spaces, improving infrastructure, and fostering a sense of safety and pride among residents. Economic stimulation is achieved by attracting tourism, encouraging local businesses, and creating markets for local artisans and services. These goals are interconnected, each feeding into and supporting the others, creating a cycle of sustainable development and cultural enrichment.

Highlighting Benefits

The benefits of revitalizing historic towns are manifold and extend beyond the observable improvements in infrastructure. Economically, revitalization can transform a town into a nexus of attraction for tourists and investors alike, leading to increased business opportunities and heightened property values. Socially, these projects foster a renewed sense of community pride and belonging as residents see the places they live in not just preserved but cherished and enhanced. Culturally, revitalization acts as a bridge between generations, making historical education a tangible experience and encouraging a shared stewardship of heritage. Each benefit feeds back into the community, creating a loop of continuous improvement and engagement.

Case Studies

Consider the revitalization of the Gaslamp Quarter in San Diego, California. Once a rundown area of the city, it underwent significant revitalization in the 1980s and 1990s. Today, it is a bustling historic district showcasing Victorian-era buildings alongside modern amenities and hosting vibrant cultural events that draw locals and tourists. This example is a testament to the transformative power of well-planned revitalization efforts. It illustrates not only the preservation of architectural gems but also the economic and social revitalization that can occur when history and modernity coalesce effectively.

By examining these foundational aspects of town and historic revitalization, you are equipped to appreciate not only the com- plexities involved in such undertakings but also the profound impacts they can have on a community's economic, social, and cultural fabric. As we move forward, keep these themes in mind, for they are the threads that weave through the success stories of towns reborn through revitalization.

1.2 The Role of Preservation in Community Identity and Sustainability

When we consider the tapestry of a community, its historic buildings are not merely structures; they are the repository of stories, the backdrop of daily life, and the physical manifestation of identity. Preserving these buildings does far more than maintain old stones and timbers; it reinforces a community's identity and instills a collective sense of pride. Each restored facade and repurposed building acts as a mirror reflecting the community's history and values back to its residents and visitors. This reflection fosters a deep-rooted connection to place, which is essential in an era where globalization could render our locales indistinguishable. For instance, when a historic theater in a small town is restored to its former glory, it becomes more than just a venue; it becomes a shared point of pride, a place where generations connect, and a cornerstone of community identity. This preservation tells residents and visitors alike that this place values its history and, by extension, its future.

The narrative of revitalization as a form of sustainable development expands as we delve into the environmental benefits of repurposing existing structures. In an age where sustainability is paramount, the choice to restore rather than demolish and rebuild aligns closely with ecological stewardship. Repurposing buildings reduces the demand for new materials, decreasing the carbon footprint associated with mining, manufacturing, and transporting construction resources. Moreover, maintaining the existing built environment minimizes urban sprawl, preserves natural landscapes, and supports the eco- logical balance. For example, converting an old mill into a mixed-use development conserves the embodied energy of the original structure and avoids the extensive environmental costs of new construction. This approach saves historical buildings and promotes an environmentally sustainable future by making the most of our existing resources.

Furthermore, the economic advantages of preservation are significant and multifaceted. Revitalizing historic sites attracts tourism, a key revenue source that supports local businesses and services. Tourists drawn to unique historical sites spend money, boosting everything from local eateries to boutique shops, supporting local economies. Additionally, preservation and revitalization projects often lead to job creation in construction, restoration, and tourism management. Beyond these immediate benefits, there is a ripple effect where preserved historic districts attract new businesses that seek the charm and foot traffic these areas offer. These businesses bring additional jobs and create a cycle of economic growth and stability that reinforces the value of investment in preservation.

The social cohesion facilitated by revitalized historic sites is one of the most compelling aspects of preservation. Historic sites often become the heart of a community's social life, hosting events, celebrations, and public gatherings that strengthen social bonds. These sites offer a venue for residents to meet, interact, and collaborate, which is crucial for fostering strong community ties and a sense of belonging. Renovating a historic waterfront can transform it from a neglected area into a bustling public space where festivals, markets, and concerts unite the community. Such transformations are not just about beautifying spaces; they are about creating venues for public joy and interaction that knit the fabric of the community tighter together.

Preservation, therefore, is not just about maintaining what is old; it's about invigorating community identity, championing sustainability, spurring economic growth, and enhancing social cohesion. These elements are interconnected, each feeding into and reinforcing the others, creating a robust framework for community vitality that stands the test of time. As we continue to explore the dynamics of town and historic revitalization, these themes will recur, underscoring the profound impact that thoughtful preservation can have on our communities.

1.3 Economic and Social Impacts: Making the Case for Revitalization

Revitalization breathes new life into a town's economy, fostering a growth climate that benefits property owners, business operators, and residents alike. When historic buildings and districts are given attention and care, they transform into hubs of activity that attract visitors and locals, driving up the demand for nearby real estate. Property values in revitalized areas often see a marked increase, providing substantial financial benefits to local homeowners and investors. This enhancement in property value also benefits local governments through increased property tax revenues, which can then be reinvested into further community development projects. Furthermore, revitalization projects stimulate local businesses by increasing foot traffic in commercial areas. Shops, restaurants, and service providers all experience a boost in patronage when situated in a vibrant, aesthetically pleasing neighborhood. This increased activity not only helps existing businesses flourish but also attracts new entrepreneurs eager to capitalize on the growing market. An example of this can be seen in cities like Pittsburgh, where the revitalization of the historic Market Square has led to a burgeoning scene of eateries, retail shops, and cultural events, drawing crowds and fostering a thriving business environment.

The potential for job creation through revitalization efforts extends well beyond the construction phase, although that phase itself is a significant source of employment. Skilled laborers, from carpenters and electricians to painters and landscapers, find ample opportunities in projects that aim to restore historic facades, update infrastructures, and convert old buildings to new uses. Beyond construction, there are lasting job opportunities in the businesses that fill these revitalized spaces, from retail associates and restaurant staff to managerial and administrative roles. Moreover, ongoing maintenance and security services are often needed, which further adds to job creation. Consider the revitalization of the waterfront area in Chattanooga, Tennessee, which not only created numerous construction jobs but also led to permanent positions in the new businesses and recreational facilities that emerged, significantly reducing local unemployment rates.

Revitalization also profoundly enhances the quality of life for community residents. By converting dilapidated areas into clean, safe, and beautiful spaces, revitalization projects contribute to a greater sense of well-being and community pride. These areas often include new or improved amenities such as parks, playgrounds, and public squares encouraging physical activity and social interaction. Furthermore, introducing cultural centers, museums, and galleries adds to the community's cultural richness, providing residents with educational and leisure opportunities. For instance, the transformation of New York City's High Line from an unused rail track into a public park has become a favorite leisure destination and a cultural venue hosting art installations and performances, greatly enhancing the quality of urban life for its residents.

The role of revitalization in fostering community engagement cannot be overstated. As areas are rejuvenated, they often become the focal points for community activities, celebrations, and civic engagement. This involvement can lead to a strengthened community identity and a collective effort to maintain and improve the neighborhood. Successful revitalization projects depend on active participation from local residents, business owners, and stakeholders, and this collaboration often continues once projects are completed. The revitalization process itself can act as a catalyst, inspiring residents to take pride in their community and to become more involved in local governance and volunteer activities. For example, following a devastating tornado in the small town of Greensburg, Kansas, the town's extensive revitalization efforts focused on sustainable building practices and green energy. This not only transformed the town into a modern, eco-friendly community but also galvanized residents around a shared vision, leading to high levels of local participation and a renewed sense of community pride.

As we reflect on these discussions, it becomes clear that the impact of revitalization extends far beyond the mere physical refurbishment of buildings. The economic and social revitalization that accompanies the restoration of historic sites fosters a vibrant community geared towards sustainable growth and enriched communal life. These transformations, marked by increased economic opportunities, enhanced quality of life, and robust community engagement, underline the powerful ripple effects of revitalization efforts across towns and cities. As such, the case for revitalization is not just about preserving the past; it's about building a foundation for a prosperous and cohesive future.

Chapter 2: Starting Points for Revitalization Projects

As you venture further into town and historic revitalization, understanding where to begin forms the crux of your journey. This chapter is designed to walk you through the critical early stages of any revitalization project, focusing specifically on the pivotal task of identifying and selecting potential sites. The decisions made here set the tone for the entire project, influencing everything from community involvement to the final outcomes. Choosing the right site is not merely a matter of finding a location in disrepair; it involves a nuanced approach that considers historical significance, community impact, and long-term feasibility. Let's explore how to navigate these initial yet decisive steps in your revitalization efforts.

2.1 Identifying Potential Sites for Revitalization and Their Historical Significance

Site Selection

Selecting a site for revitalization is akin to setting the founda- tions for a house. Just as a strong foundation supports a home against the elements, a well-chosen site forms the bedrock of a successful revitalization project. When identifying potential sites, consider a blend of historical value, strategic location, and potential for community impact. Historical value might be evident through the architectural uniqueness or the site's role in local heritage, making it a candidate for preservation and a focal point for community pride. The location is equally crucial; it should enhance accessibility, visibility, and integration into the broader urban or town fabric. Lastly, consider the potential impact on the community. A site with significant potential for positive social, economic, or cultural impact can galvanize community support and contribute to the project's sustainability.

Assessing Historical Significance

Understanding a site's historical significance requires a detailed assessment that goes beyond the surface. This involves evaluating the architectural value, which includes the design, craftsmanship, and materials that signify historical periods, styles, or cultural influences. Moreover, it delves into the history of events associated with the site and its cultural importance to the community. Was it a hub for significant historical events? Does it hold a symbolic value for local residents? These aspects of historical significance enrich the revitalization project's narrative and enhance its acceptance and resonance within the community.

Community Input

Involving the community early in the site selection process is not just beneficial; it is essential. Community input ensures that the project aligns with local values, addresses community needs, and taps into local knowledge and history, which might not be immediately apparent to external project teams. Engaging with community members can be achieved through public forums, direct consultations, and participatory decision-making processes. This inclusion helps build a sense of ownership and support among community members, laying a foundation for collaborative efforts as the project progresses.

Feasibility Studies

Once potential sites are identified and their historical significance assessed, conducting feasibility studies is the next critical step. The studies evaluate the practical aspects of revitalization projects. They look into the structural integrity of buildings, the availability of required technologies, the alignment with regulatory frameworks, and the financial viability. Feasibility studies should also consider potential environmental impacts and propose mitigation strategies if necessary. This thorough analysis helps foresee challenges and planning effectively, ensuring that the revitalization efforts are grounded in reality and have a higher chance of success.

Reflective Exercise: Evaluating Potential Sites

To practically apply these concepts, consider this exercise: Choose a site in your community or a known historical site that interests you. Reflect on its architectural features, historical relevance, and location. Discuss with peers or jot down how this site could impact the community if revitalized. What challenges might arise in its revitalization? This exercise will help you think critically about the factors involved in site selection and prepare you for similar assessments in your revitalization projects.

2.2 Building a Revitalization Team: Roles and Responsibilities

Assembling a team for a town and historic revitalization project is much like forming a diverse orchestra where each member plays a distinct yet harmonious role, contributing to the overall success of the endeavor. The composition of this team is crucial, as it brings together varied expertise that spans different fields, each critical to the nuanced demands of revitalization projects. A well-structured team typically includes project managers, historians, architects, and community liaisons, each bringing unique skills and perspectives to the table.

Project managers act as the conductors of this orchestra, overseeing the project from conception to completion. They ensure that all activities are aligned with the project's goals, manage resources efficiently, and keep the project on schedule and within budget. Their role involves a high level of coordination, and communication, as they must effectively connect all team members and stakeholders, promptly addressing any issues. Historians are the custodians of the project's cultural integrity. They provide essential insights into the site's historical significance and advise on preserving its heritage throughout the revitalization process. Their expertise ensures that the renovations respect and reflect the site's past, making the project not only a redevelopment but also a restoration of history.

Architects bring the vision of the revitalization to life, marrying functionality with aesthetic and historical accuracy. They design the structures in a way that both preserves the old and accommodates the new, ensuring that any additions or alterations enhance rather than detract from the buildings' original character. On the other hand, community liaisons serve as the vital link between the project team and the local residents. They facilitate communication, relay community concerns and feedback to the project managers, and help incorporate local insights into the planning and execution phases. This role is pivotal in building and maintaining public trust and support, which are indispensable for the project's acceptance and success.

Allocating responsibilities among these team members is a strategic process that demands a clear understanding of each role's scope and the project's requirements. While overseeing the project's progress, the project manager might delegate specific tasks like budget tracking or timeline management to assistant managers. Historians might be tasked not only with research but also with documenting the changes for future records. Architects could be responsible for initial drafts and overseeing the construction phase to ensure the designs are followed accurately. Community liaisons would organize and manage community engagement activities and provide ongoing dialogue between the project team and the public. This clear delineation of responsibilities ensures that the project progresses smoothly and efficiently, with each team member able to focus on their strengths and contribute effectively.

Consulting with external experts in preservation, urban planning, and economic development throughout the project can provide additional layers of insight and expertise.

These experts can offer specialized knowledge that might be absent within the core team, such as legal advice on heritage laws, advanced technical solutions for preservation, or innovative economic models to fund the revitalization. Their input can be invaluable in navigating complex challenges requiring spe- cialized knowledge or validating the project approach against current industry standards and practices.

Including community representatives in the team is not just beneficial but essential for ensuring that the revitalization project aligns well with the needs and expectations of local residents. These representatives bring a voice to the table that reflects the community's aspirations, concerns, and ideas. Their involvement ensures that the project fosters a sense of community ownership and pride rather than feeling like an imposition from external forces. It also helps preemptively address potential resistance or objections, as community rep- resentatives can help negotiate solutions acceptable to both the project team and the local population. Their ongoing in- volvement in the project can aid in maintaining public support and enthusiasm, which are crucial for the project's long-term success and sustainability.

By carefully building and managing a diverse and skilled project team, you set the stage for a successful revitalization project in the physical renovation, fostering community development and historic preservation. This careful orchestration of roles and responsibilities ensures that every aspect of the project is approached with expertise, consideration, and respect for the community's heritage and future.

2.3 Engaging the Community Early: Strategies for Inclusive Planning

In the early stages of a revitalization project, engaging the community enriches the process and ensures that the outcomes reflect the community's needs and aspirations. Public meetings are among the most effective forums for initiating this engagement. These gatherings serve as critical platforms where ideas are shared, feedback is gathered, and a collective vision begins to take shape. Holding these meetings in accessible locations ensures broad participation, which is vital for the inclusive nature of the project. During these sessions, presenting clear, concise information about the project's goals, potential impacts, and expected benefits helps demystify the process for residents and stakeholders. It's crucial that these meetings are not just informative but also interactive. Encouraging questions, suggestions, and discussions not only fosters a sense of community ownership but also uncovers unique local insights that might not be otherwise captured.

Beyond public meetings, surveys and questionnaires offer a structured way to gather input from those who might not attend public gatherings. These tools can reach a broader audience, ensuring that diverse segments of the community have the opportunity to contribute their views. The design of these surveys should be straightforward and respectful of the respondents' time while being comprehensive enough to gather meaningful data. Digital platforms can significantly increase reach and ease of distribution, but alternative formats like paper surveys might be necessary to ensure inclusivity for all community members, regardless of their access to technology. The insights gathered from these surveys are invaluable, providing quantifiable data to guide decision-making and highlight areas requiring more focused attention.

Moreover, organizing collaborative workshops can be a transformative approach to community engagement. These workshops are designed to be hands-on, involving community members directly in the planning process. By working together in small groups, participants can delve deeper into specific aspects of the revitalization project, from design elements to sustainable practices. Facilitators can guide these discussions, ensuring the conversation remains productive and focuses on constructive outcomes. The collaborative nature of these workshops yields creative solutions and strengthens community bonds—people feel more connected to a project when they have had a hand in shaping it.

Transparent communication is the thread that ties all these engagement strategies together. Maintaining openness about the project's progress, challenges, and changes is essential for building and sustaining trust with the community. This means regular updates through various channels—whether it be newsletters, social media posts, or community bulletin boards. Transparency isn't just about sharing successes; it's also about honesty in facing setbacks and being transparent about how they will be addressed. This ongoing dialogue reassures the community that their input is valued and that they are respected partners in the revitalization process.

Reflective Prompt: Community Engagement Plan

Consider drafting a preliminary community engagement plan for a hypothetical revitalization project. Identify the methods you would use to engage different community segments, considering factors like age, technology access, and cultural backgrounds. Outline potential topics for public meetings, critical questions for a survey, themes for collaborative workshops, and strategies for transparent communication. This exercise will help you visualize how comprehensive community engagement can be structured to foster inclusivity and collaboration.

As this chapter concludes, we've explored the foundational strategies for engaging with your community early in the revitalization process. From the democratic platforms of public meetings to the targeted inquiries of surveys and the collaborative nature of workshops, each element plays a significant role in weaving the rich tapestry of community input into the revitalization project. Transparent communication acts as the continuous thread that maintains the project's integrity and the community's trust. As we transition to the next chapter, these themes of inclusivity and collaboration will continue to be pivotal, guiding the project from planning to execution with the community at its heart. The journey ahead promises to transform physical spaces and the communal bonds that define them.

Chapter 3: Navigating Challenges in Preservation

As you delve deeper into the intricacies of town and historic revitalization, you'll inevitably encounter many challenges, each demanding a nuanced approach and strategic thinking. Securing adequate funding emerges as a pivotal hurdle that can dictate the pace and scope of your project. This chapter aims to equip you with the knowledge and tools to navigate the financial landscapes of preservation, helping you transform potential obstacles into stepping stones toward successful revitalization.

3.1 Funding Your Project: A Guide to Grants, Loans, and Crowdfunding

Understanding Funding Options

The quest for funding can often feel like navigating a labyrinth, where each turn presents new options and decisions. Understanding the various funding sources available is your first step towards demystifying this complex journey. Federal and state grants are often the most sought-after sources, as they do not require repayment and can provide substantial financial support for your projects. These grants are typically awarded based on specific criteria, which may include the historical significance of the site, the projected benefits to the community, and the project's overall feasibility. Loans, while needing repayment, offer another viable route, especially when immediate funding is required to kickstart or continue work without delays. These are often provided by banks, private lenders, or through government-backed programs that offer lower interest rates and more favorable terms for community projects.

Crowdfunding has emerged as a powerful tool in the digital age, democratizing the funding process by allowing anyone to contribute financially to your project. Platforms like Kick-starter and GoFundMe enable you to reach a global audience, share your vision, and garner support from individuals who share your passion for preservation. This method not only raises funds but also builds a community of supporters who are invested in the success of your project.

Application Strategies

Applying for grants requires a strategic approach that aligns your project's objectives with the goals of the grantor. Begin by thoroughly researching potential grants to ensure your project meets the eligibility criteria. When preparing your application, focus on clearly articulating the benefits your project will bring to the community. This could include economic revitalization, educational opportunities, or enhanced community identity and pride. Be specific about the outcomes you aim to achieve and support your claims with data and research where possible. Demonstrating alignment with the grantor's objectives is crucial; show how your project will help fulfill their mission or contribute to their goals. This strategic alignment not only strengthens your application but also positions your project as a worthy investment for the funding body.

Crowdfunding Campaigns

Launching a successful crowdfunding campaign hinges on your ability to communicate the story and significance of your project compellingly. Start by setting realistic financial goals based on a detailed budget that outlines how funds will be used. This transparency builds trust with potential donors and gives them a clear understanding of the project's scope and impact. Create engaging multimedia content—videos, images, and compelling narratives—that bring your project to life and connect emotionally with viewers. Regular updates and active engagement on your crowdfunding page keep supporters involved and motivated to help you reach your funding goals. Offering creative rewards for different levels of donations can also incentivize contributions, making supporters feel they are receiving something valuable in return for their investment.

Leveraging Tax Incentives

Tax incentives and credits are often overlooked, but they are potent tools that can significantly reduce the overall cost of preservation projects. These incentives are designed to encourage the preservation of historic properties by making them financially advantageous for property owners and developers. Familiarize yourself with federal tax credits available for historic preservation, which can cover a substantial percentage of the rehabilitation expenses. State and local governments may also offer additional incentives, including property tax reductions or discounts. To maximize these benefits, consult a tax advisor specializing in historic preservation to ensure you fully understand the application process and compliance requirements. Leveraging these tax incentives effectively can make a significant difference in your project's financial viability, turning the daunting costs of preservation into manageable expenses.

Reflective Exercise: Mapping Your Funding Strategy

To apply these concepts, consider creating a funding map for a potential or ongoing revitalization project. List all possible funding sources, including grants, loans, and crowdfunding platforms. For each, note key application deadlines, eligibility criteria, and strategic tips specific to that source. Assess the potential amount each source could contribute and how it aligns with your project's phases and needs. This exercise will not only help you visualize your funding landscape but also prioritize your efforts to secure financial support efficiently.

Navigating the financial aspects of historic preservation requires creativity, perseverance, and strategic planning. As you explore the various funding avenues, remember that each project is unique, and successfully securing funds often in- volves tailoring your approach to fit your project's specific characteristics and needs. With a clear understanding of the options available and strategies to leverage them effectively, you are well-equipped to turn the vision of revitalization into a tangible, funded reality.

3.2 Balancing Historical Integrity with Modern Needs

Adaptive reuse stands as a cornerstone strategy for those intent on breathing new life into historical structures while ensuring they meet the needs of today's society. This approach involves repurposing old buildings for contemporary use without stripping them of their historical essence. It's a practice that not only preserves cultural landmarks but also contributes to sustainability by reducing the demand for new construction materials and minimizing urban sprawl. For example, an old factory may be transformed into a mixed-use development that includes residential spaces, retail areas, and offices while maintaining the original architectural features that give the building its unique character. This process requires a delicate balance, demanding a deep understanding of both the struc- ture's historical significance and the functional requirements of modern buildings. The key here is to work closely with architects and historians from the outset to devise a design that respects the past, perhaps by preserving iconic elements like original brickwork or timber beams, while integrating modern infrastructure such as energy-efficient heating systems and contemporary plumbing solutions that fit seamlessly into the existing framework.

Navigating building codes and regulations presents another layer of complexity in the revitalization of historic structures. Modern building standards, which are primarily concerned with safety, accessibility, and energy efficiency, can often be at odds with the preservation of old architectural styles and materials. To address this, you must engage in what can be described as a regulatory balancing act. This involves collaborating with local authorities to explore possible exemptions or modifications to standard building codes that allow for preserving historical features. For instance, while a complete overhaul of an electrical system in a historic building might be necessary to comply with current codes, other less intrusive adaptations, like using hidden wiring solutions that do not damage the original plasterwork, might also be acceptable. It's about finding solutions that fulfill safety and functionality requirements without compromising the building's historical integrity. Engaging a consultant specializing in historic preservation can prove invaluable in these situations, providing expert advice on navigating the maze of regulations while respecting the building's heritage.

The challenge of balancing the expectations of diverse stakeholders must be addressed. Each group involved in a revitalization project—from preservationists and local government officials to business owners and residents—has its own expectations and objectives. Preservationists may prioritize the utmost integrity of historical features, while business owners might be more concerned with functionality and modern amenities that attract customers. Meanwhile, local residents could be focused on how the project impacts community cohesion and local heritage. Successfully managing these differing priorities requires open, ongoing communication and a participatory approach to project planning. Workshops and regular meetings where stakeholders can voice their concerns and contribute ideas are essential. These discussions help identify common ground and clarify the practical implications of various choices, thereby fostering a collective decision-making process that respects both the heritage and the future of the community.

Incorporating sustainable practices into revitalization projects has become a preference and necessity in today's environmentally conscious world. Sustainability in historic preservation goes beyond energy efficiency; it encompasses the use of environmentally friendly materials and practices reduce the carbon footprint of the building throughout its renovation and subsequent use. For instance, using recycled materials to restore floors or walls preserves the historic look and feel and promotes resource efficiency. Additionally, installing solar panels on rooftops or incorporating rainwater harvesting systems can modernize these historic properties without altering their appearance significantly. The goal is to ensure that these buildings not only tell the story of their past but also contribute positively to environmental conservation efforts. This approach aligns with global sustainability goals and enhances the building's appeal and functionality, making it a viable part of the community's progress into the future.

3.3 Addressing Gentrification: Ethical Revitalization Practices

Understanding the dynamics of gentrification is crucial as you navigate the complexities of revitalizing historic towns and neighborhoods. Gentrification often starts when revitalized areas attract new, typically more affluent, residents due to the improved quality of life and amenities. While this can lead to economic uplift, it can also result in increased property values, which, while seemingly beneficial, can lead to the displacement of long-standing, lower-income residents. This displacement can erode the cultural fabric and community networks that give neighborhoods unique character and vitality. Recognizing these potential impacts, it becomes essential to approach revitalization with strategies that enhance physical spaces and protect and empower existing communities.

One of the most effective ways to ensure revitalization benefits all residents is through inclusive development practices. At the heart of these practices is the commitment to creating opportunities that allow existing residents to enjoy the fruits of new developments without the threat of displacement. This can be achieved through initiatives like affordable housing programs, which ensure that a percentage of new or renovated housing remains accessible to lower-income residents at below-market rates. Another powerful strategy is the implementation of local hiring practices. These practices prioritize the employment of residents in both the construction phase and the new businesses that are set up in the revitalized areas, thereby circulating the economic benefits within the community and enhancing residents' stakes in the project's success.

Community Benefits Agreements (CBAs) are formal agreements between developers and coalitions of community organizations, ensuring that redevelopment projects confer benefits to local residents, not just developers. CBAs include commitments to provide community spaces, support local schools, fund community services, or adhere to environmental standards. to provide community spaces, support local schools, fund community services, or adhere to environmental standards. These agreements are negotiated through a process that involves significant community input, ensuring that the voices of the residents are not only heard but have a direct impact on the development outcomes. The enforceability of CBAs adds a layer of accountability, making them a robust tool for ensuring that revitalization projects deliver real, measurable benefits to the communities they aim to serve.

Ongoing monitoring and evaluation play pivotal roles in maintaining the integrity and effectiveness of revitalization efforts. By establishing clear metrics and regular assessment intervals, stakeholders can track whether the projects meet their intended social, economic, and cultural objectives or if unintended consequences, such as gentrification, are occurring. This continuous evaluation allows for the adjustment of strategies in real-time, ensuring that the projects remain aligned with community needs and expectations. Effective monitoring involves not only the quantitative tracking of economic indicators but also qualitative assessments through community feedback and participation. This holistic approach ensures that revitalization remains a dynamic, responsive process, truly reflective of the community's evolving aspirations.

As this chapter wraps up the discussion on the ethical complexities of revitalization, remember the broader implications of your efforts. Each step taken towards renewing a historic site or neighborhood doesn't just reshape buildings—it redefines the home of a community. The strategies discussed here aim not just to preserve bricks and mortar but to foster environments where communities thrive amidst change. As we move forward, the insights garnered here will lay the groundwork for exploring innovative funding and resource management strategies in the next chapter, ensuring that your revitalization projects are culturally and socially responsible, financially viable, and sustainable

Chapter 4: Innovative Funding and Resource Management

Navigating the financial terrains of town and historic revitalization requires passion and a profound understanding of the myriad funding mechanisms that can fuel these transformative endeavors. As we delve into this chapter, we will uncover the potent financial tools at your disposal, focusing particularly on tax credits and incentives— a somewhat underexploited reservoir of fiscal support for heritage conservation. If leveraged wisely, these financial instruments can significantly reduce project costs and enhance the economic feasibility of preserving our architectural legacies.

4.1 Leveraging Tax Credits and Incentives for Historic Preservation

Exploring Federal and State Programs

Navigating the labyrinth of federal and state tax credits designed specifically for historic preservation projects can initially seem daunting. These financial incentives are crafted to encourage the preservation and reuse of historic buildings as integral parts of economic revitalization. Understanding how to navigate and apply for these programs is crucial. For example, the Federal Historic Preservation Tax Incentives program includes a 20% tax credit for the certified rehabilitation of historic structures. This is a significant boon for developers, offering a dollar-for-dollar reduction in owed federal taxes.

Similarly, many states offer complementary incentives, which can be combined with federal credits for even more significant financial relief. To effectively tap into these resources, you must familiarize yourself with the specific eligibility criteria, which often hinge on the property's historical significance and the nature of the renovations planned. Engaging with state historic preservation offices early in your project planning can provide guidance and critical insights that streamline the application process.

Maximizing Financial Benefits

Maximizing the financial benefits of tax credits and incentives requires a strategic approach, often involving combining different funding sources. This strategy not only enhances the financial viability of projects but also opens up opportunities to scale up the scope and impact of revitalization efforts. For instance, pairing federal tax credits with local tax abatement programs or grants can cover a substantial portion of the project costs. Additionally, understanding the timing of these incentives is crucial; often, the financial benefits are realized incrementally over several years, which needs to be accounted for in your project's financial planning. Consulting with financial experts specializing in historic preservation projects is advisable to optimize the benefits. They can provide insights into effective financial structuring and help navigate the complexities of combining various forms of financial assistance.

Case Examples

To illustrate the practical application and impact of these tax credits, consider the restoration of the historic Pullman District in Chicago. This project, which revitalized a significant landmark area, utilized both federal and state tax credits to restore numerous buildings to their former glory, simultaneously boosting the local economy through increased tourism and job creation. The project leaders successfully navigated the application process for these credits, which involved meticulous documentation of the historical significance of the structures and detailed accounting of the rehabilitation expenses. The financial impact was profound, with the project costs substantially offset by the tax credits, thereby enhancing the project's overall feasibility and sustainability.

Challenges and Solutions

While the benefits of tax credits are substantial, the path to securing them is often fraught with challenges. One common hurdle is stringent compliance with the Secretary of the Interior's Standards for Rehabilitation. These standards, which ensure that renovations preserve the historic character of buildings, can often be restrictive and require innovative solutions to meet modern needs without compromising historical integrity. The application process can also be cumbersome, requiring detailed documentation and sometimes lengthy approval times. To navigate these challenges, engaging with preservation consultants who can provide expertise in historic rehabilitation and ensure that project plans meet all necessary standards is beneficial. Moreover, building a good relationship with local historic preservation officers can facilitate a smoother review and approval process. These officials can provide preliminary feedback before formal submission, allowing you to refine your application to align with regulatory expectations.

In this exploration of tax credits and incentives, we uncover the pathways to accessing these funds and the strategic considera- tions necessary to harness their potential fully. As we continue to explore innovative funding and resource management strate- gies in the subsequent sections, keep in mind the critical role of comprehensive planning and expert collaboration in realizing the financial strategies that support your revitalization goals.

4.2 The Power of Public-Private Partnerships in Revitalization

When venturing into town and historic revitalization, the synergy created through public-private partnerships (PPPs) can often be the linchpin for success. These collaborations harness the unique strengths and resources of both public and private sectors to achieve outcomes that might be beyond the reach of any single entity. Crafting successful partnerships involves a clear understanding of the roles and expectations of each party. Typically, the public sector provides regulatory support and may offer financial incentives or infrastructure investments, while the private sector contributes funding, expertise, and innovation. Setting these roles early, with transparent agreements and legal frameworks, is crucial to align the visions and objectives of all stakeholders involved. This foundational alignment ensures that the partnership op- erates based on mutual benefit and shared goals, significantly enhancing the project's chances for success.

The benefits of engaging in PPPs for revitalization projects are manifold. One of the most significant advantages is the pooling of resources. Financial burdens and risks are shared, reducing the weight on any single participant and broadening the scope of feasible projects. For instance, a city might partner with a private developer to restore a historic neighborhood, with the town providing tax incentives and the developer contributing the necessary capital and construction expertise. This shared risk and resource model not only accelerates project completion but also enhances the quality and sustainability of the development. Moreover, PPPs combine diverse expertise, from urban planning and historical preservation to financial management and marketing. This convergence of knowledge fosters innovative solutions that respect historical integrity while ensuring modern relevance and functionality.

Drawing from real-world applications, consider the revitalization of the historic Pearl District in Portland, Oregon, which blossomed from a PPP. Initially an industrial zone, the area was transformed into a vibrant mixed-use neighborhood through a partnership between the city and private developers. The collaboration was structured through clear roles, with the town upgrading infrastructure and providing tax breaks while developers handled the construction and management of new commercial and residential spaces. The outcome was a resounding success, resulting in a bustling urban district that maintained its historic charm while offering modern amenities and green spaces. This project boosted local economic growth and became a national model for sustainable urban development.

Best practices for managing and maintaining PPPs throughout the lifecycle of a revitalization project involve continuous communication and flexible management structures. Regular meetings and updates ensure that all parties remain aligned with the project's progress and emerging challenges. Establishing conflict resolution protocols from the outset is crucial to address disagreements constructively without derailing the project. Maintaining public engagement and transparency can also foster broader community support, contributing to the project's legitimacy and success. Effective management of these partnerships requires a balance of firm contractual agreements and the flexibility to adapt to new circumstances or opportunities, ensuring the partnership remains robust and productive over time.

In navigating the complexities of revitalization efforts, the strategic formation and nurturing of public-private partnerships stand out as a dynamic and effective approach to breathing new life into historic spaces. By combining resources, expertise, and the shared commitment of both public and private sectors, these partnerships catalyze sustainable developments that honor our past while building for the future. As we continue exploring innovative funding and resource management strategies, the lessons gleaned from successful PPPs provide valuable insights into the collaborative potential to drive transformational change in our communities.

4.3 Crowdfunding Success Stories: Lessons Learned

Introduction to Crowdfunding

In the evolving landscape of funding for historic preservation projects, crowdfunding has emerged as a dynamic and accessible tool. This method leverages the power of the crowd— individuals who collectively contribute small to substantial amounts of money through an online platform— to support various initiatives. Crowdfunding platforms like Kickstarter, Indiegogo, and GoFundMe have broadened the funding horizons for projects that might not meet the strict criteria required by traditional funding sources like grants and loans. These platforms offer various models, from donation-based systems, where contributors give money without expecting anything in return, to reward-based systems, where backers receive tangible items or experiences in return for their contributions. Each model presents unique opportunities and challenges, but the core advantage remains the same: engaging a broad audi- ence and harnessing the collective enthusiasm and resources of supporters from around the globe.

Designing a Successful Campaign

The cornerstone of a successful crowdfunding campaign is its ability to tell a compelling story. This narrative should do more than outline the need for funds; it should evoke emotions and illustrate the project's impact. For historic preservation, this might involve sharing the history of the site, its significance to the community, and the potential transformation that can be achieved with the backers' support. High-quality videos and images showcasing the site's beauty and historical importance can enhance this storytelling, making the project come alive for potential donors. In addition to a compelling narrative, offering well-thought-out rewards can significantly boost the appeal of your campaign. These rewards should scale with the donation size, ranging from small tokens like thank-you postcards or digital wallpapers for small contributions to more substantial rewards like invitations to exclusive opening events or personalized tours for more significant donations. Effective promotion is also vital to reach a broad audience. Utilizing social media, local media, community newsletters, and email campaigns can help spread the word about your crowdfunding campaign, drawing in more supporters and increasing the chances of achieving your funding goal.

Analyzing Success Stories

To understand what drives a successful crowdfunding campaign, let's examine specific cases where preservation projects not only met but surpassed their funding targets. One notable example is the campaign to restore a historic cinema in a small town. The project set out to raise $50,000 to repair and update the aging interior while preserving its iconic Art Deco facade. Through a well-orchestrated campaign highlighting the cinema's role in the town's cultural life and memories, the project captured the community's heart and the interest of cinema enthusiasts globally. The campaign offered rewards like free movie tickets, named seats, and even a private screening event for higher-tier donations. By the end of the campaign, they had raised over $70,000, allowing them to expand their restoration plans. The success factors here were deeply rooted in engaging storytelling, attractive rewards, and robust promotional efforts that utilized both social media and community events to generate buzz and foster a sense of ownership among backers.

Post-Campaign Strategies

After a successful crowdfunding campaign, maintaining momentum and fulfilling commitments to backers are crucial to sustaining support and trust. This involves regular updates about the project's progress, including both triumphs and setbacks. Such transparency ensures backers feel valued and reassured of the impact of their contributions. Fulfilling rewards as promised is also crucial; delays in delivering rewards can lead to dissatisfaction and might deter backers from supporting future projects. Consider ways to keep the community engaged post-campaign for ongoing or phased projects. Options include setting up a dedicated website or social media group where supporters can follow the project's progress, participate in discussions, and even contribute further ideas and resources. This sustained engagement helps keep the community invested in the project's success and builds a lasting relationship that can be beneficial for future preservation efforts.

As this chapter on innovative funding and resource management draws to a close, we reflect on the diverse strategies that can bolster financial support for historic preservation. Each method offers unique benefits and challenges, from leveraging tax incentives and forging public-private partnerships to tapping into the power of the crowd. What remains clear is that the successful financing of preservation projects often requires a combination of these strategies tailored to the specific needs and circumstances of the project. As we turn the page to the next chapter, we carry forward the insights and lessons learned here, ready to explore the equally crucial aspects of community engagement and mobilization in the context of historic revitalization.

Chapter 5: Community Engagement and Mobilization

Imagine stepping into the heart of your town's historic district, where every building whispers tales of yesteryears and every cobblestone bears the marks of generations past. Here, the past meets the present, and the future is shaped not by mere chance but by the collective will and concerted efforts of the community. This chapter delves into the pivotal role of community engagement in the revitalization process, where your role transcends being a mere spectator to becoming an active participant in scripting the next chapter of your town's heritage.

5.1 Tools and Tactics for Effective Community Outreach

The success of any revitalization project hinges significantly on how well the community is engaged. Effective community outreach begins with a clear understanding of who your stakeholders are. Stakeholders in a historic revitalization project typically include local residents, business owners, historians, local government officials, and potential investors. Each of these groups has a vested interest in the project, but their perspectives and expectations can vary widely. Identifying and categorizing these stakeholders allows you to tailor your outreach efforts effectively. For instance, local residents may be primarily concerned with how the project will affect property values and the local culture, while investors might focus more on the economic potential of the project. Recognizing these nuances is crucial in addressing the concerns and harnessing the enthusiasm of all parties involved.

Once stakeholders are identified, the next step is to establish robust communication channels. Traditional town hall meetings have long been the cornerstone of community engagement, of- fering a public forum for presenting plans, gathering feedback, and fostering a sense of community involvement. However, in today's digital age, social media platforms, websites, and email newsletters are just as crucial for reaching a broader audience. These online platforms are invaluable for providing regular updates, soliciting input, and keeping the community engaged throughout the project's lifecycle. For example, creating a dedicated project

Facebook page or Instagram account can not only keep the community informed but also serve as a vibrant space for discussions and suggestions, making the engagement process more dynamic and interactive.

Engaging stakeholders meaningfully requires more than just opening lines of communication; it requires actively encouraging participation and investment in the project. Engagement strategies can include interactive surveys that allow stakeholders to express their preferences for certain design elements, community contests to name new amenities, or open forums where community members can voice their ideas and concerns. These strategies not only ensure that stakeholders feel heard but also that they are co-creators of the project, fostering a deeper connection and commitment to the revitalization efforts.

Measuring the effectiveness of these engagement efforts is vital to ensure that the strategies employed are indeed working and to make necessary adjustments. Tools such as engagement metrics on social media, meeting attendance records, and the quantity and quality of feedback received through surveys can provide tangible data on how engaged the community is. Regularly assessing this data allows you to fine-tune your approach, perhaps by increasing outreach in areas where engagement is low or by introducing new engagement strategies if current efforts are not resonating as well as expected.

Reflection Exercise: Community Engagement Evaluation

Take a moment to reflect on a local project or initiative you were part of or aware of. Think about the engagement strategies that were used. Were they effective? How did the community respond? What could have been done differently to enhance stakeholder involvement? Jot down your thoughts or discuss them with peers. This reflection can provide personal insights into the practical applications of community outreach strategies, enriching your understanding and approach to community engagement in your own revitalization projects.

As we continue to explore the layers of community engagement and mobilization, remember that at the core of these efforts is the profound respect for the community's voice. Each step taken to engage the community not only enriches the project but also strengthens the town's social fabric, ensuring that the revitalization efforts are deeply rooted in its people's collective aspirations and cherished heritage.

5.2 Organizing Community Workshops and Visioning Sessions

When embarking on revitalizing historic areas, the mosaic of community voices forms the cornerstone of every decision and action. Organizing community workshops and visioning sessions is akin to opening a dialogue with the soul of the town, where each participant contributes to painting a collective vision of the future. These gatherings are not merely meetings; they are incubators for ideas, solutions, and shared dreams. To ensure these sessions are successful, meticulous planning and preparation are paramount. It begins with setting clear objectives for each session—what do you hope to achieve? Is it generating ideas, gathering feedback, or making decisions on specific aspects of the revitalization project? Once objectives are set, selecting the right venue becomes crucial. It should be a space that is accessible to all community members, reflective of the town's heritage, and conducive to open, creative discussions. Preparing materials and resources that stimulate discussion and inspire creativity is also essential. These might include maps, plans, historical data, and visual aids that help participants fully visualize potential changes and their impacts.

Facilitating these sessions requires a skillful blend of leadership and empathy. As a facilitator, one must navigate a spectrum of perspectives, balancing diverse opinions and steering conversations toward constructive outcomes. Techniques such as active listening, where you give full attention to the speakers and acknowledge their ideas, help in building an atmosphere of trust and respect. Employing round-robin techniques can ensure that everyone has a chance to voice their thoughts without the more vocal participants dominating the session. Additionally, setting ground rules at the start of the session can foster a respectful and inclusive environment. These rules might include no interruptions, criticism of ideas, not individuals, and an emphasis on building on others' suggestions. Such a structured yet flexible approach to facilitation helps in managing the dynamics of the group, ensuring that the sessions are productive and harmonious.

Capturing ideas and feedback effectively during these sessions is crucial for translating community input into actionable insights. One effective method is using visual recording or graphic facilitation, where a facilitator visually maps out the discussion in real-time. This keeps the participants engaged and helps synthesize complex information into understandable, memorable formats. Utilizing digital tools like online surveys or interactive apps during the session can also provide immediate data that can be analyzed quickly and efficiently. Additionally, appointing a note-taker or using a voice recorder can ensure no valuable insights are lost. After the session, organizing the collected data into themes or categories related to specific aspects of the revitalization project helps identify critical priorities and common concerns that require attention.

The ultimate goal of these workshops and visioning sessions is to weave community input into the fabric of the revitalization plans. This integration requires a thoughtful analysis of the collected ideas and feedback, assessing them not just for their popularity but for their impact on the project's goals and feasibility. Prioritizing these inputs and turning them into elements of the project plans involves continuous dialogue with the community, ensuring that the decisions reflect their needs and aspirations. This might involve several iterations of the plans, each refined through further community consultations. By maintaining this iterative dialogue, the community remains engaged and invested in the revitalization process, seeing their fingerprints on every aspect of the project's evolution.

In essence, community workshops and visioning sessions are more than just strategic tools for gathering input; they are a testament to the power of collective community action. Through careful planning, empathetic facilitation, meticulous capture of ideas, and thoughtful integration of community feedback, these sessions can turn the hopes and dreams of a community into tangible plans that guide the revitalization of their historic spaces. As we move forward, these foundational engagements inspire trust and cooperation and foster a shared commitment to revitalizing not just buildings but the very heart of the community.

5.3 Utilizing Digital Platforms for Community Engagement and Feedback

In an era where digital interaction is as commonplace as face-to-face conversations, leveraging digital tools for community engagement presents a dynamic approach to involving a broader demographic in the revitalization process. Digital platforms, ranging from social media networks to specialized project management tools, provide unparalleled opportunities to reach out, engage, and gather feedback from community members who might not be accessible through traditional methods. These tools are not just about broadening reach; they introduce a level of interactivity and immediacy to the engagement process, enhancing the quality and quantity of community feedback and participation.

The selection of digital tools is crucial and should align with the specific needs of the project and the community's digital accessibility. For instance, platforms like Facebook and Twitter are excellent for reaching a wide audience, while tools like SurveyMonkey or Google Forms can facilitate detailed surveys and polls. For more targeted discussions, platforms like Slack or dedicated forums can be set up to foster deeper dialogue among community members. Additionally, interactive websites dedicated to the project can serve as central hubs where updates, events, and data are shared, and feedback is systematically gathered. These digital venues offer the advantage of allowing participants to engage at their convenience, which can significantly increase participation rates and provide a richer, more diverse pool of community input.

Creating interactive content is key to captivating and maintaining the community's interest. This involves designing content that is not only informative but also engaging and easy to interact with. Videos, for instance, can be highly effective in telling the story of the project, showcasing the potential transformations, and illustrating the impact of community involvement. These can be supplemented with interactive elements such as clickable timelines, before-and-after sliders for proposed changes, and virtual tours of the historic sites. Interactive infographics can also be used to simplify complex data about the project's benefits, timelines, or budget allocations. The goal is to make the content as engaging as possible, encouraging community members to consume the information, share it, and provide feedback.

Virtual workshops and meetings have become increasingly popular, particularly in scenarios where face-to-face interactions are limited. These virtual gatherings can be just as effective as in-person meetings if managed well.

Platforms like Zoom, Microsoft Teams, or Google Meet can host these sessions, and with features like breakout rooms, polls, and Q&A sessions, they can be highly interactive. The benefits of hosting virtual workshops include higher attendance rates, reduced costs, and the ability to record sessions for later viewing. Preparing for these sessions involves ensuring all participants have access to the necessary technology and are familiar with the platform. This might mean providing tutorials or tech support prior to the meeting to ensure everyone can participate effectively. During the sessions, it's essential to keep the dialogue focused and inclusive, ensuring that all voices are heard and that the digital space remains respectful and constructive.

Analyzing feedback from these digital platforms is integral to shaping project development in a way that genuinely reflects the community's needs and preferences. Digital tools offer the advantage of easily quantifiable data, whether it's the number of likes, shares, comments on social media posts, or the responses to digital surveys and polls. This data can be used to gauge the community's interest and sentiment about different aspects of the project. More sophisticated tools like sentiment analysis software can further dissect the feedback from social media or website comments to understand the community's emotions and concerns more deeply. This analysis helps make informed decisions about the project, ensuring that the community's input is gathered and pivotal in steering the project's course.

As this chapter on utilizing digital platforms for community engagement concludes, we see how these modern tools can significantly enhance the interaction between project developers and the community. By effectively using digital platforms to reach out, engage, and gather feedback, the revitalization process becomes a more inclusive and dynamic endeavor. The insights gained from digital engagement not only enrich the project but also ensure that it remains aligned with the community's aspirations and concerns, paving the way for a revitalization effort that truly reflects the community's heart and soul.

As we transition into the next chapter, we will carry forward the valuable lessons learned about engaging digitally with communities, further exploring how these digital interactions can be seamlessly integrated into broader strategies for successful historic revitalization.

Chapter 6: Practical Applications and Case Studies

6.1 Adaptive Reuse Projects That Transformed Communities

Imagine walking through a neighborhood where old, unused industrial buildings have been transformed into vibrant community hubs, bustling with cafes, art galleries, and tech startups. This is the power of adaptive reuse, a concept that redefines the possibilities of preservation and community revitalization. Adaptive reuse refers to the process of repurposing old buildings for new uses while maintaining their historical integrity. This practice not only preserves architectural heritage but also breathes new life into communities, making it an essential strategy in the arsenal of urban development.

One of the critical success factors of adaptive reuse projects lies in their ability to marry innovative design with the original character of the building. Architects and planners play a pivotal role here, creatively integrating modern functionalities while respecting the building's historical elements. For instance, the transformation of a century-old factory into a modern office space requires a deep understanding of both the structural and aesthetic qualities of the building. The challenge is to ensure that new interventions like glass partitions or modern lighting solutions complement rather than overshadow the rustic charm of exposed brick walls and wooden beams.

Community support is another cornerstone of successful adaptive reuse projects. When local residents and businesses are involved in the planning process, it not only garners public support but also ensures that the development aligns with the community's needs and aspirations. This participatory approach helps create spaces that truly serve the public, whether as cultural centers, public libraries, or commercial complexes. Engaging the community early in the decision-making process fosters a sense of ownership and pride, which is crucial for the long-term success and sustainability of the project.

Diverse Examples of Adaptive Reuse

Across the globe, adaptive reuse projects have shown remarkable success in revitalizing neighborhoods and supporting sustainable development. A notable example is the transformation of the old Ghirardelli Chocolate Factory in San Francisco into a bustling marketplace and hotel. This project not only preserved a beloved city landmark but also created a vibrant public space that attracts tourists and locals alike, contributing significantly to the local economy.

Another inspiring example is found in the heart of New York City, where the High Line, an abandoned rail track, was transformed into an elevated urban park. This project is a testament to innovative urban renewal, turning a derelict infrastructure into a green oasis in the city, thus improving the quality of urban life and boosting property values in the surrounding areas.

In smaller communities, adaptive reuse can also play a trans- formative role. For instance, converting an old school building into a community health center in a rural town not only preserved a historic structure but also addressed a critical community need for accessible health services. This project demonstrates how adaptive reuse can contribute to community health and well-being while maintaining cultural heritage.

Lessons Learned

From these case studies, several valuable lessons emerge for future adaptive reuse projects. First, the importance of thorough planning and feasibility studies cannot be overstated. These preliminary steps help identify the building's structural challenges and opportunities, guiding the design and development process.

Second, the integration of sustainable practices in adaptive reuse projects enhances their environmental and social value. Incorporating energy-efficient systems, sustainable materials, and green spaces can turn old buildings into sustainability models, setting a standard for future developments.

Third, continuous community engagement throughout the project—from planning to implementation—ensures that the development remains responsive to the needs of the community. This ongoing dialogue helps adapt the project to changing circumstances and maintain public support.

Adaptive reuse projects offer a compelling narrative of trans-formation and sustainability. They tell stories of how places that once thrived in the past can be reimagined for a prosperous future, making them not just spaces of nostalgia but beacons of innovation and community life. As we delve deeper into the practical applications of town and historic revitalization, these examples and lessons provide a foundation of understanding and inspiration, guiding our ongoing efforts to rejuvenate and preserve our cherished urban landscapes.

6.2 Grassroots Efforts Leading to Large-Scale Change

In the vibrant tapestry of community revitalization, grassroots efforts often act as the crucial threads that bind together individual aspirations for a collective transformation. These initiatives, born from the community's own desire for change, highlight the profound power of local action in shaping environments that foster a deeper sense of belonging and pride. When communities take charge of their revitalization projects, it does more than alter physical spaces; it redefines the community's role in their own narratives of development and renewal.

Empowering communities to lead their revitalization efforts involves more than just encouraging participation; it requires providing them with the tools, knowledge, and support necessary to envision, plan, and execute these transformations. This empowerment process often begins with education and capacity-building workshops where community members are trained in the basics of urban planning, heritage preservation, and project management. These training sessions demystify the complexities of revitalization efforts and equip residents with the skills needed to take active roles in their community's development. Another effective method is to facilitate planning sessions that help translate community concerns and ideas into actionable projects. These sessions can be guided by professionals but should be led and owned by community members, ensuring that the outcomes reflect their needs and visions. By empowering communities in this way, revitalization efforts become more sustainable and rooted in the local context, reflecting the true identity and aspirations of the residents.

Building Momentum

Building momentum behind grassroots initiatives requires a dynamic approach that captures and sustains the community's interest and commitment. Organizing community events is a powerful strategy to generate enthusiasm and participation.

These events, whether workshops, festivals, or public exhibitions, serve as platforms for sharing information, celebrating local culture, and showcasing the benefits of revitalization efforts. For example, a festival organized in a recently revitalized public square can demonstrate the potential of similar projects elsewhere in the community, inspiring others to support or initiate new projects. Such events also provide opportunities to celebrate local successes, which can boost community morale and the momentum behind ongoing efforts.

Leveraging local media is another effective way to build momentum. By engaging with newspapers, radio stations, and even local bloggers and social media influencers, grassroots initiatives can reach a wider audience, drawing attention to their efforts and attracting more community members to their cause. Media coverage can help validate the community's efforts, attract local celebrity endorsements, or even garner support from local businesses, all of which can add credibility and appeal to the project. Regular updates on the progress of revitalization projects, featured in local media outlets, keep the community informed and engaged, maintaining the momentum that is so critical for the sustained success of these initiatives.

Case Studies

Examining specific case studies where grassroots efforts have catalyzed significant revitalization projects offers invaluable insights into the mechanisms and impacts of such initiatives.

One poignant example comes from a small town that rallied to save and repurpose its historic train station, which was on the brink of demolition. Led by a local heritage group that started with small fundraising events and heritage walks, the campaign quickly gained traction. The group used social media to share stories of the station's historical significance and its potential as a community space. This strategic use of digital platforms reached a broad audience, eventually attracting funding and support from local businesses and the municipal government. Today, the restored station serves as a vibrant community center, hosting art classes, a small museum, and a café operated by local entrepreneurs. The success of this project has ignited further interest in preserving other historic sites in the town, demonstrating how targeted grassroots efforts can lead to broader community revitalization.

Sustaining Efforts

Sustaining grassroots efforts over time is crucial for ensuring that the initial enthusiasm translates into long-term impact and continuous community involvement. Establishing formal structures, such as community development corporations or neighborhood associations, can provide ongoing leadership and governance for revitalization initiatives. These organizations can oversee the management of completed projects and the planning of new ones, keeping the community engaged and the momentum alive. Additionally, securing diverse funding sources, including membership dues, grants, and revenue from community-owned enterprises, can provide the financial stability needed to support ongoing activities and future projects.

Moreover, fostering a culture of recognition and celebration plays a significant role in sustaining grassroots efforts. Recognizing individual volunteers, community leaders, and supportive businesses through public acknowledgments, awards, or feature stories in local media can boost morale and encourage continued participation. Celebrating milestones and successes not only reinforces the value of the community's efforts but also inspires further involvement and support, ensuring that the revitalization efforts not only begin with the community but are also sustained by it, continuing to flourish and evolve as vibrant expressions of the community's resilience and creativity.

6.3 Overcoming Regulatory Hurdles: A How-To Guide

Navigating the complex terrain of regulations is a critical step in revitalizing historic towns and buildings. Regulatory hurdles such as zoning laws, preservation ordinances, and building codes can often seem daunting. These laws are designed to protect the historical integrity, safety, and planned development of urban and rural areas, but they can also pose significant challenges for revitalization projects that aim to bring modern functionalities to historic settings. Understanding these regulations, and how to effectively navigate them, is crucial for ensuring that your revitalization projects not only start off on the right foot but also move smoothly towards completion.

One of the most common regulatory challenges in historic revitalization involves zoning laws. These laws dictate how properties in certain areas can be used, affecting everything from building height and density to the types of businesses operating in a particular area. On the other hand, preservation ordinances are specifically designed to protect the architectural and historical integrity of buildings and neighborhoods. While these regulations are vital for maintaining the character of historic areas, they can restrict the types of modifications that can be made to a building. For example, a preservation ordinance might require any renovations to preserve the façade of a historic building, complicating efforts to modernize the structure. Navigating these regulations requires a thorough understanding of the specific laws applicable to the area and the project. Researching local zoning laws and preservation ordinances early in the planning process can help identify potential roadblocks and guide the design and development phases to align with regulatory requirements.

Strategies for Success

Successfully navigating regulatory hurdles often involves proactive engagement with the relevant regulatory bodies. Early and consistent communication with these authorities can facilitate a smoother approval process for your revitalization projects. It's beneficial to schedule preliminary meetings with local planning departments, historic preservation boards, and other relevant entities as soon as project goals are defined. These dialogues allow you to present your vision, gather valuable feedback, and understand the regulatory framework from the perspectives of those who enforce it. In many cases, regulatory bodies are willing to work with developers to find mutually agreeable solutions that allow for modernization while preserving historical value.

Seeking variances or exemptions is another strategy that can effectively overcome regulatory hurdles. Variances allow for deviations from standard zoning requirements under certain conditions, which can be crucial for projects that aim to bring innovative uses to historic properties. The process of applying for a variance typically involves presenting a case that demonstrates why the variance is necessary for the project's success and how it will benefit the community. Exemptions, particularly those related to preservation ordinances, can sometimes be obtained if it can be demonstrated that strict compliance would result in practical difficulties or unnecessary hardships that would hinder the revitalization efforts.

Collaboration with Authorities

Building a collaborative relationship with local authorities can significantly enhance the likelihood of project approval and success. This collaboration can take many forms, from joint planning sessions and workshops to regular project updates and consultations. By involving regulatory bodies in the planning process, you can gain allies who deeply understand the regulatory landscape and can provide insights that refine project plans to better meet regulatory standards. Moreover, these authorities can become advocates for the project within the government, helping to navigate bureaucratic processes and expedite approvals.

Case Studies

A compelling example of successful navigation of regulatory hurdles is revitalizing an old warehouse district into a mixed-use residential and commercial area. The project faced significant challenges due to strict zoning laws that did not initially allow for residential use in the area. By engaging with city planners and the local community early in the process, the developers demonstrated the potential benefits of the project, including increased economic activity and improved community safety. Their proactive approach led to a rezoning of the area, which allowed the project to proceed and ultimately transformed the district into a thriving part of the city.

Another case study involves the restoration of a historic theater that was initially hindered by preservation ordinances requiring the retention of certain architectural features that were no longer structurally sound. The project team worked closely with the local historic preservation board to devise a plan that allowed for the replication of these features using modern materials that mimicked the original appearance while ensuring safety and durability. This solution satisfied the preservation requirements while allowing the revitalization to move forward, resulting in a successful restoration that maintained the theater's historical integrity and appeal.

These case studies illustrate that while regulatory hurdles can be daunting, they are not insurmountable. With strategic planning, proactive engagement, and collaborative problem-solving, it is possible to navigate these challenges effectively and successfully complete revitalization projects.

As we close this chapter on overcoming regulatory hurdles, we reflect on the importance of understanding and strategically navigating the complex regulations governing historic revitalization projects. From zoning laws to preservation ordinances, the regulatory landscape can significantly influence the scope and success of these endeavors. By engaging early and often with regulatory bodies, seeking variances or exemptions when necessary, and fostering collaborative relationships with authorities, you can navigate these hurdles effectively. This proactive approach ensures compliance and facilitates smoother project execution, ultimately contributing to revitalizing historic towns and buildings that honor their past while embracing the future.

The next chapter will explore integrating modern amenities into historic sites, seamlessly incorporating contemporary features into historic settings to enhance functionality without compromising historical integrity. This exploration will continue to build on the foundational knowledge and strategies discussed so far, providing you with further insights and tools to manage and execute your historic revitalization projects successfully.

Chapter 7: Integrating Modern Amenities in Historic Sites

As we step into the heart of revitalizing our cherished historic sites, the challenge often lies not just in preserving the echoes of the past but in weaving the conveniences of the modern age into the rich tapestry of history. This delicate balance asks us to respect and retain the timeless charm of these sites while ensuring they meet contemporary standards of functionality and sustainability. Integrating modern amenities, particularly green technologies, into historic sites represents a profound commitment to heritage and environmental responsibility. It's an endeavor that enhances the usability and relevance of these spaces and aligns with broader goals of sustainable development and conservation.

7.1 Green Technologies in Historic Preservation

Innovative Solutions

The task of integrating cutting-edge green technologies into historic sites is as complex as it is rewarding. Imagine a centuries-old building, its walls a witness to history, now harnessing the power of solar energy without the addition of intrusive modern fixtures. Such innovations are made possible through the thoughtful application of building-integrated photovoltaics (BIPV) technologies. These systems allow photo-voltaic materials to be incorporated seamlessly into building elements such as the roof, skylights, or facades, thus preserving the aesthetic integrity while contributing to energy efficiency. Another groundbreaking technology is geothermal heating and cooling systems, which utilize the earth's stable underground temperature to regulate the climate in buildings. By installing these systems, historic properties can enjoy modern heating and cooling solutions with minimal visual impact on their structure and surroundings.

Case Studies

Successful examples of these technologies applied in historic settings provide a blueprint for what is possible. Consider the case of a Victorian-era museum in London that implemented a BIPV system in its glass roof. The system not only preserved the visual elegance of the historic glasswork but also transformed the roof into an energy-generating asset, significantly reducing the museum's carbon footprint.

Another compelling example is found in a historic courthouse in Virginia, where a geothermal system was installed within the existing framework of the building. This system provided an energy-efficient solution to heating and cooling, avoiding the aesthetic disruption that conventional HVAC systems might have caused.

Best Practices

When selecting and implementing green technologies in historic preservation projects, several best practices should be followed to meet sustainability and preservation goals. First, it is crucial to conduct a thorough assessment of the historic site to understand its structural and historical constraints. This assessment should guide the selection of technologies that are compatible with the physical and aesthetic characteristics of the building. Engaging with specialists in historic preservation technology early in the process can provide insights into innovative solutions that respect the site's heritage. Additionally, it's important to involve local preservation authorities to ensure that all modifications comply with relevant regulations and guidelines.

Challenges and Solutions

Introducing modern green technologies into historic settings is not without its challenges. One of the most significant hurdles is the potential conflict between the preservation of original building materials and the installation requirements of new technologies. For instance, installing solar panels on a historic slate roof may require modifications that could threaten the roof's integrity and appearance. To address these challenges, solutions such as using non-invasive mounting systems that do not require drilling into the original materials can be effective. Another common challenge is the higher upfront costs associated with customizing technologies to fit historic sites. Here, accessing specialized grants and funding programs designed to support green initiatives in historic preservation can be crucial.

Reflective Section: Evaluating Potential for Green TechnologyIntegration

Consider a historic site you are familiar with or involved in preserving. Reflect on the structure's characteristics, historical significance, and current energy consumption patterns. What green technologies could be suitable for this site? How would you address the potential challenges of integrating these technologies into the historic fabric? This exercise encourages you to apply the concepts discussed and envision practical applications that respect both the past and the future.

As we continue to explore the integration of modern amenities into historic sites, the journey reveals a landscape where respect for heritage and commitment to sustainability coexist. Through innovative solutions, detailed case studies, and adherence to best practices, we discover that modernizing historic sites with green technologies not only preserves these treasures but also redefines them as exemplars of environmental stewardship. As you move through the spaces of history, transformed yet untouched in their essence, the fusion of old and new unfolds not just as an architectural achievement but as a testament to our evolving relationship with our past and our planet.

7.2 Achieving ADA Compliance in Historic Structures

Navigating the intricate requirements for ADA (Americans with Disabilities Act) compliance in historic structures is a task that marries the necessity of accessibility with the reverence for architectural heritage. For anyone involved in preserving and revitalizing historic sites, understanding and implementing ADA standards isn't just about adhering to legal requirements— it's about extending the life and relevance of these spaces to everyone, regardless of physical ability. This dual focus on accessibility and preservation challenges you to think creatively about respecting the past while accommodating everyone who might visit or use a historic site today.

Regulatory Requirements

The ADA sets guidelines to ensure public spaces are accessible to people with disabilities. These standards cover a wide range of physical accommodations, including wheelchair access, Braille signage, and accessible restroom facilities. When these standards are applied to historic buildings, the challenge intensifies due to the structural and design limitations inherent in older constructions. For instance, adding an elevator or ramp to a centuries-old building can be complex if the original architecture includes narrow doorways, multiple small steps, or delicate materials that cannot be easily modified. Moreover, there are instances where compliance might threaten the building's historical integrity or cause irreversible changes to its character-defining features. In such cases, the ADA does provide certain allowances for historic properties, acknowledging that not every feature will be feasible to adapt. The key is to consult with the State Historic Preservation Office (SHPO) and the ADA National Network early in your planning process to understand which standards are absolute and where exceptions might be granted. This consultation can provide clarity and direction, helping you navigate the complex intersection of accessibility laws and historic preservation guidelines.

Sensitive Adaptations

Adapting historic sites to meet ADA standards while maintaining their historical character requires a thoughtful, innovative approach. One effective strategy is the use of reversible modifications. These are changes that improve accessibility but can be removed in the future without significant damage to the original structures. For example, adding a ramp made from materials that complement the building's exterior can provide necessary access without permanent alterations to the building. Another approach is the use of technology to enhance accessibility. Audio guides, virtual tours, and interactive apps can provide rich, accessible experiences for visitors who might not otherwise be able to physically access certain parts of a historic site. These technological adaptations preserve the physical integrity of the site while opening up its historical and cultural riches to a broader audience.

Success Stories

Across the globe, numerous success stories of historic sites have gracefully integrated ADA standards. A prominent example is a 19th-century courthouse in the Midwest that underwent significant adaptations to become fully accessible. The project involved installing an elevator and accessible restrooms and adjusting doorways and hallways to accommodate wheelchairs. Despite these extensive modifications, the project team worked diligently to match new materials with the original ones, preserving the building's historic character. The impact of these adaptations has been profound, not only in terms of compliance but also in making the courthouse a more inclusive public space that welcomes all members of the community.

Another inspiring example comes from a small, historic theater in New England. The theater introduced specialized seating areas for wheelchair users, enhanced auditory systems for the hearing impaired, and gentle ramps that blended seamlessly with the existing structure. These adaptations were carefully planned to ensure that they did not detract from the theater's historic charm. The theater has since reported a significant increase in visitors, including those who previously could not access the venue, illustrating the social and economic benefits of thoughtful ADA compliance.

Resources and Support

A wealth of resources and support is available for project managers navigating the complexities of making historic sites ADA-compliant. Numerous grants specifically aimed at improving accessibility in historic settings can provide financial assistance for such projects. Organizations like the National Endowment for the Humanities and various disability advocacy groups offer funding opportunities that can help cover the costs of adaptations. Additionally, technical assistance is available from ADA National Network Centers, which guide compliance requirements and practical adaptation strategies. Engaging with these resources early and often can ease the financial and logistical burdens associated with ADA compliance, ensuring that historic sites can be enjoyed by everyone, now and in the future.

In weaving together the threads of accessibility and preservation, you are not merely modifying a building; you are expanding its relevance and ensuring its legacy continues robustly into the future. This chapter underscores the delicate dance between honoring the past and embracing inclusive futures, guiding you through practical strategies and inspiring examples that showcase what is possible when we commit to making history accessible to all.

7.3 Smart Cities and Historic Preservation: Finding the Balance

In an era where technology permeates every facet of our lives, integrating smart city technologies into the preservation of historic sites offers an intriguing challenge: how can we enhance functionality and visitor experience without diluting the historical essence that makes these places significant? This delicate balance requires thoughtful strategies that embrace modern innovations while staunchly safeguarding our cultural heritage. As we explore this integration, it becomes clear that the potential for technology to amplify the educational and experiential aspects of historic sites is boundless, provided we approach it with sensitivity and creativity.

Smart city technologies, which range from IoT (Internet of Things) sensors to advanced data analytics, can transform historic sites into more interactive and accessible spaces. Imagine a historic building where sensors monitor environmental conditions to prevent deterioration or where augmented reality (AR) apps allow visitors to see not only the current state of the building but also to visualize its past, peopled with historical figures and furnished with period decor. These technologies do not merely add a layer of modernity; they deepen the visitor's engagement with the site, providing a richer understanding of its historical context. However, the integration of such technologies must be handled with care to ensure that they complement rather than overshadow the historic character of these sites. For instance, AR implementations should be designed to be unobtrusive, with visitors accessing features through their smartphones or other personal devices, ensuring that the physical integrity and aesthetic of the site remain unaltered.

Balancing innovation with preservation is akin to walking a tightrope. On one side lies the risk of overwhelming the historical ambiance with high-tech interventions; on the other, the opportunity to bring history to life in ways that resonate with a tech-savvy generation. This balance can be achieved by involving heritage professionals from the outset in the planning and implementation of technology solutions. Their insights can ensure that technological enhancements amplify the site's historical narrative rather than detract from it. Additionally, adopting a phased approach to technology integration can help. Starting with pilot projects allows stakeholders to assess the impact of new technologies on the visitor experience and the physical site, making adjustments as needed before full-scale implementation.

Turning to case examples, some cities have already begun to chart a course in integrating smart technologies with historic preservation. In one European city, a medieval fortress has been equipped with sensor technology that monitors structural stability and environmental conditions, providing data that helps in the maintenance and preservation of the site. Another example is an ancient aqueduct where visitors use an app to access multimedia narratives that tell the story of the aqueduct's construction and use throughout history.

These cases exemplify how technology can be used to enhance the educational value of historic sites while ensuring their preservation for future generations.

The future directions for the coexistence of smart city initiatives and historic preservation are promising. As technology continues to evolve, so too will the ways in which we can apply it to the preservation of our cultural heritage. The key will be to leverage these advancements to preserve and breathe new life into historic sites, making them relevant and accessible to a broader audience. This might include using machine learning algorithms to predict and mitigate potential damage to historic structures or employing virtual reality (VR) to recreate historical events at specific sites, providing a fully immersive experience that educates and captivates visitors.

As we close this exploration into integrating smart city technologies with historic preservation, we recognize the delicate balance between innovation and the preservation of our cultural heritage. By employing thoughtful strategies, engaging heritage professionals, and adopting a phased approach, we can ensure that technology serves as a bridge connecting the past to the present and future. Looking forward, the potential to enhance visitor experiences through these technologies invites us to imagine a world where history is preserved not behind glass cases but within the very fabric of our daily lives, made vivid and vital through the wise use of technology. As we transition into the next chapter, we carry forward the lessons learned here, ready to explore further the role of environmental sustainability in historic preservation.

Chapter 8: Addressing Environmental and Sustainability Concerns

The imperative of sustainability profoundly affects our practices and choices as we endeavor to preserve the historical integrity of our cherished landmarks. This chapter invites you to explore how environmental considerations are not just adjunct elements but core aspects of historic preservation. By integrating sustainable practices, we ensure that our endeavors to safeguard the past also contribute positively to our ecological future, thus maintaining a delicate balance between heritage conservation and environmental stewardship.

8.1 Sustainable Materials for Historic Preservation

When stepping into the world of historic preservation, the materials used are not merely substances to repair or replace what time has worn away; they are threads in the fabric of history — each selection either strengthens or diminishes the integrity of this tapestry. Sustainable materials in historic preservation are those that meet the needs of the present without compromising the ability of future generations to experience and appreciate our cultural heritage. The selection of these materials involves a meticulous assessment of their environmental impact, compatibility with historic preservation standards, and the practical aspects of sourcing and logistics.

Material Selection

Choosing the right materials is pivotal in ensuring that the restoration efforts are both effective and respectful to the original architecture. Sustainable materials for historic preservation must align with the building's historical context, meet current environmental standards, and ensure longevity and durability. Materials such as lime-based plasters and mortars, which have been used for centuries, continue to be favored in restoration projects for their compatibility with traditional masonry. These materials are not only historically accurate but also breathable, allowing moisture to evaporate naturally, which is crucial for the health of historic buildings. Similarly, reclaimed wood, salvaged from dismantled buildings or fallen timbers, can be used for repairs and replacements, preserving the aesthetic continuity while reducing the demand for new lumber and the associated environmental depletion.

Environmental Impact

The environmental impact of materials used in historic preservation extends beyond the immediate concerns of energy consumption and greenhouse emissions. A comprehensive approach involves life cycle assessments (LCAs) that evaluate the environmental impact of a material from extraction and processing through to its end of life. For instance, the production of traditional lime plaster emits significantly less carbon dioxide compared to cement-based products. By choosing materials with lower environmental impacts, preservation efforts can contribute to broader sustainability goals, such as reducing the carbon footprint and minimizing waste.

Success Models

The use of sustainable materials is beautifully illustrated in the restoration of the Farnsworth House, a historic site in Illinois. In addressing the deterioration of its iconic steel elements, the conservation team opted for low-carbon, recycled steel for replacement parts. This choice not only preserved the architectural integrity of this modernist icon but also demonstrated a commitment to environmental sustainability. Another example is the use of recycled glass and ceramic tiles in restoring historic interiors, which provides durability and style while incorporating materials that would otherwise contribute to landfill waste.

Sourcing and Logistics

The practical aspects of sourcing sustainable materials involve a careful consideration of their origin, the energy used in transportation, and the availability in sufficient quantities. Prioritizing local sources reduces transportation emissions and supports local economies, further aligning the restoration projects with sustainable development goals. Moreover, understanding the supply chains and the availability of these materials can influence project timelines and budgets. For instance, sourcing reclaimed wood locally not only ensures a lower carbon footprint but also provides material that is acclimatized to the local environment, reducing the risk of warping or deterioration.

Reflective Exercise: Assessing Material Choices

Consider a historic preservation project you are familiar with, or imagine a hypothetical one. Reflect on the building materials used or proposed. Were they sustainable? How did or could these choices impact the environment and the authenticity of the historic site? This reflection can deepen your understanding of the intersection between sustainability and preservation, encouraging a more conscientious approach in future projects.

In weaving sustainability into the very fibers of our preservation efforts, we ensure that the stories told by our historic sites endure not just in memory and stone but also in the legacy of environmental stewardship they embody. As we continue to explore the nuances and challenges of integrating sustainability into preservation, let us remain committed to choices that honor both our past and our planet.

8.2 Energy Efficiency Solutions for Historic Buildings

In historic preservation, marrying the old with the new in terms of technology presents challenges and opportunities. The introduction of innovative technologies designed to enhance energy efficiency is a testament to our evolving capabilities to safeguard our architectural heritage while embracing sustainable practices. These technologies are crafted to weave seamlessly into the fabric of historic structures, ensuring they do not undermine the aesthetic or structural integrity that makes these buildings invaluable.

One of the most significant advancements in this area is integrating HVAC systems tailored to historic buildings' unique needs. Traditional heating, ventilation, and air conditioning systems can be obtrusive and often require alterations that compromise a building's historical integrity. However, newer models are designed to be less invasive and more adaptable to the constraints of historic properties. For instance, ductless systems can be installed without opening up walls for ductwork, preserving the original materials and designs of historic interiors. Similarly, high-velocity, small-duct HVAC systems can be used to provide modern heating and cooling solutions with minimal visual impact. These systems use small, flexible ducts that can be threaded through existing wall cavities, floors, and ceilings, delivering comfort without the disruptive installation process associated with traditional HVAC systems.

Another innovative technology gaining traction is the use of smart thermostats and building management systems that can optimize energy use while maintaining the microclimate conditions necessary to protect sensitive historic materials. These systems adjust the indoor climate based on real-time data. They can be programmed to maintain different conditions in separate parts of a building, which is particularly useful in large, historic museums or libraries where different collections may require different environmental conditions.

Regulatory Compliance

Navigating the maze of energy regulations and standards is critical to implementing energy efficiency solutions in historic buildings. Each geographic location has its own set of regulations that dictate energy usage, emissions, and conservation practices. When dealing with historic buildings, these regulations often intersect with preservation standards, complicating compliance. Understanding these regulations is crucial—not only to ensure legal compliance but also to benefit from any available incentives for energy-efficient upgrades. In many regions, governments offer tax breaks, rebates, and grants for energy efficiency improvements, even for historic properties, as part of broader initiatives to reduce energy consumption and greenhouse gas emissions.

Engaging with local historic preservation officers and energy regulators early in the planning process can provide guidance and facilitate a smoother path to compliance. These professionals can offer insights into how best to balance preservation requirements with energy efficiency goals and can help identify which upgrades are likely to receive approval. In some cases, they can also assist in expediting the approval processes for projects that clearly demonstrate a commitment to both preservation and sustainability.

Case Studies

Exploring case studies helps to concretize the application of energy efficiency technologies in historic settings. One notable example is the retrofit of a 19th-century government building in Washington, D.C., which was one of the first to receive LEED certification for its sustainable design and operation. The project included the installation of an advanced HVAC system, energy-efficient lighting, and the use of programmable thermostats. Despite the building's age and historical significance, the project team reduced its energy consumption by 23%, demonstrating that historic buildings can adapt to modern energy standards without sacrificing their heritage.

Another inspiring case is a historic theatre in San Francisco that underwent a major energy retrofit, including installing LED lighting and a new, efficient HVAC system. The retrofit improved the comfort of patrons and performers. It preserved the intricate plasterwork and other historic decorative elements that would have been at risk with installing a traditional HVAC system. The project was a collaboration between preservation- ists, energy consultants, and the local community, showcasing a model of stakeholder engagement that led to a successful balance of preservation and modernization.

Best Practices

In planning and executing energy efficiency upgrades in historic structures, several best practices should guide your approach. Firstly, conducting a thorough energy audit before planning upgrades is essential. This audit should assess current energy use and pinpoint areas where improvements can be made, taking into consideration the unique aspects of the historic building. Secondly, prioritizing upgrades that offer the greatest energy savings and least impact on the building's character is a strategic approach. Often, simple changes like upgrading to energy-efficient lighting and adding insulation can significantly reduce energy consumption without extensive alterations to the building. Lastly, continuous monitoring and maintenance of new systems are crucial to ensure they operate efficiently and do not adversely affect the historic fabric of the building. Regular check-ins and tweaks to the systems can prevent potential damage and help maintain an optimal balance between energy efficiency and preservation.

Navigating the complexities of integrating modern energy solutions into historic frameworks requires a delicate balance of respect for the past and commitment to the future. By embracing innovative technologies, adhering to regulatory requirements, learning from successful case studies, and following best practices, we ensure that our beloved historic buildings stand the test of time and contribute to a sustainable future. As we continue exploring the various facets of environmental sustainability in historic preservation, these insights and approaches provide a robust framework for ensuring that heritage sites can be preserved and made more energy-efficient, serving as beacons of sustainability in the modern world.

8.3 Water Conservation Practices in Revitalization Projects

In the realm of revitalizing historic sites, water conservation emerges not only as a necessity driven by environmental concerns but also as a strategic component that enhances the sustainability and longevity of these cherished landmarks. Integrating water conservation techniques into preservation projects involves a nuanced approach that respects the integrity of historic structures while employing modern ecological practices. This subchapter delves into the various water conservation techniques particularly suited for such settings, the positive impacts these practices have on preserving historic sites, the challenges encountered during their implementation, and real-life success stories illuminating the path for future projects.

Conservation Techniques

Water conservation in historic preservation projects often revolves around two main strategies: rainwater harvesting and efficient irrigation systems. Rainwater harvesting involves collecting and storing rainwater from rooftops and other surfaces to be used for various non-potable needs such as landscape irrigation, flushing toilets, and even cooling tower make-up water. This technique not only reduces reliance on municipal water supplies but also helps manage stormwater runoff, which can be particularly damaging to historic foundations and landscapes. On the other hand, efficient irrigation systems ensure that the water collected, whether from rain or municipal sources, is used with maximum efficiency. Drip irrigation systems, which deliver water directly to the base of plants, minimize evaporation and runoff, making them ideal for the delicate landscapes often found in historic sites. Soil moisture sensors and smart irrigation controllers can further optimize water usage by adjusting watering schedules based on real-time weather conditions and soil moisture levels.

Impact on Preservation

The benefits of implementing water conservation measures in historic preservation extend beyond just reduced water bills and compliance with local sustainability mandates. These practices play a crucial role in protecting the structural integrity of historic buildings. For example, properly managing stormwater through techniques like rainwater harvesting can prevent water pooling around foundation areas, a common cause of structural damage in older buildings. Additionally, maintaining a controlled landscape irrigation regime ensures that the moisture levels in the soil are kept at levels that do not threaten the foundations. Furthermore, these conservation practices contribute to the preservation of historic gardens and landscapes, which are often integral components of heritage sites, by ensuring that they receive adequate and consistent watering, even during periods of drought.

Implementation Challenges

While the benefits are clear, integrating water conservation practices into historic preservation projects is not without its challenges. One significant hurdle is the adaptation of modern systems to work within the constraints imposed by historic structures and landscapes. For example, installing a rainwater harvesting system often requires alterations to existing guttering and downspouts, which can be challenging if the goal is to preserve the original materials and appearance. Additionally, many historic sites are located in urban areas where space for large water storage tanks is limited. Solutions to these challenges require innovative thinking and careful planning. For instance, slimline tanks or underground tanks can be used where space is at a premium, and modern materials that mimic historical ones can be employed to ensure visual continuity.

87

Success Stories

The successful incorporation of water conservation techniques in historic preservation projects provides valuable lessons and inspiration. One notable example is a historic estate in Virginia that implemented a comprehensive rainwater harvesting system integrated with a drip irrigation network. The system collects rainwater from the rooftops of several buildings on the estate, stores it in a series of underground tanks, and uses it to irrigate the extensive formal gardens, which are an essential aspect of the estate's historical significance. This project not only reduced the estate's water consumption by 40% but also protected the structural integrity of its historic buildings from water damage.

Another example comes from a museum complex in New Mexico that incorporated low-impact development (LID) techniques into its landscaping. These techniques, which include bioswales and permeable pavements, help manage stormwater onsite, reducing runoff and enhancing groundwater recharge. The museum's approach not only preserves the historic site's landscape but also serves as an educational tool for visitors, demonstrating the practical application of sustainable water management practices in preserving cultural heritage.

Integrating water conservation practices in historic preservation signifies a harmonious blend of respecting our past and protecting our future. By implementing these practices, we safeguard our historic sites and contribute to the broader environmental goals of conservation and sustainability. As we close this exploration of water conservation techniques, we are reminded of the delicate balance required to maintain the integrity and essence of our heritage while embracing modern sustainability practices. This chapter sets the stage for the next, where we will explore the broader implications of sustainability in historic preservation, ensuring that our efforts today will allow future generations to enjoy and learn from these historical treasures.

Chapter 9: The Future of Preservation and Revitalization

As we step forward into the future of preservation and revitalization, we find ourselves at the intersection of heritage and innovation. It's here, amidst the whispers of the past and the rapid pulse of modern technology, that we discover virtual reality (VR) as a transformative tool in historic preservation. This technology, once relegated to the domains of gaming and high-tech research, now offers profound potential for those dedicated to the conservation of our architectural and cultural heritage. The merging of VR with preservation efforts marks a significant advancement in how we approach these projects and redefines how we interact with and experience history.

9.1 The Role of Virtual Reality in Preservation Planning

Technological Advancements

Virtual reality technology has grown by leaps and bounds, evolving from clunky headsets and simplistic environments to sophisticated systems that deliver deeply immersive experiences. In the context of preservation planning, VR is a powerful tool, enabling architects, planners, and stakeholders to step into a virtual representation of historical sites, either as they currently exist or as they might appear once restoration efforts are complete. This isn't just about seeing a building restored to its former glory; it's about experiencing it—walking its halls, viewing the intricacies of its craftsmanship, and understanding the spatial dynamics that photographs or blueprints can never fully convey. For preservation efforts, this means stakeholders can make more informed decisions, experiencing the impact of potential changes firsthand, thus ensuring that every modification serves both the site's heritage and its future needs.

Enhancing Visitor Experience

Beyond the planning stages, VR dramatically enhances how people experience historic sites. Imagine donning a VR headset and being transported back in time, walking through an ancient Roman marketplace, or standing in the heart of a bustling medieval castle. This technology can bring history to life, providing context and narrative that enrich the visitor experience far beyond what static displays or guided tours can offer. For educational purposes, this means that students and visitors aren't just told what happened in a space; they're shown in a compelling, immersive format that engages their senses and emotions. The educational content delivered through VR not only increases understanding but also fosters a deeper appreciation of cultural heritage, making history accessible and engaging for a generation raised in a digital world.

Planning and Design

In the planning and design phases of preservation projects, VR proves invaluable for its ability to present detailed visualizations not just to architects and planners but also to the local community and stakeholders involved. This inclusive approach is crucial, as it allows for a shared vision to emerge — a collective agreement on the future of a historic site that respects its past while making it relevant and sustainable for the future. VR simulations can show various design options, compare them side by side, and adjust elements in real-time, providing a dynamic platform for collaboration and creativity. Moreover, these visualizations can help secure funding and approvals, as decision-makers and potential donors can see and experience their investment's impact before a single stone is moved.

Case Studies

The practical application of VR in historic preservation is vividly illustrated by several pioneering projects around the globe. One notable example is the restoration of the historic Fort York in Toronto, Canada, where VR was used to simulate the fort's appearance both before and after the proposed renovations. This allowed for a thorough public review and input, ensuring the community played a role in shaping the final outcome. Another example can be found in the ancient city of Palmyra, Syria, where VR has been used to recreate structures that were destroyed by conflict, preserving these vital cultural assets for future generations in a digital format. These case studies not only underscore the practical benefits of VR in preservation efforts but also highlight its potential to foster a deeper connection between people and their cultural heritage.

Interactive Element: Virtual Walkthrough

To further illustrate the transformative power of VR in historic preservation, consider engaging in a virtual walkthrough of a site currently undergoing restoration. This interactive experience, accessible via a simple VR app and headset, can offer a firsthand look at the restoration process, blending before-and-after visuals with historical facts and narrative insights. This exercise enhances your understanding of the site's historical significance and demonstrates the practical application of VR technology in bringing these spaces to life.

Integrating technologies like VR offers exciting possibilities as we continue to navigate the future of preservation and revitalization. It propels us into an era where history is not merely observed but experienced, where architectural treasures are not just restored but reimagined, and where every individual can step through the annals of time and witness history in the making. This is more than preservation; it's a renaissance of our cultural heritage, fueled by innovation and driven by a commitment to celebrate and conserve the legacies of our past.

9.2 Crowdsourcing for Preservation: A New Era of Community Involvement

In the dynamic landscape of historic preservation, the emergence of crowdsourcing has marked a significant shift towards more inclusive and participatory approaches. This method leverages the power of the collective—engaging a broad community online to contribute financially, intellectually, and creatively to preservation projects. Crowdsourcing is not merely about pooling financial resources; it's a multifaceted engagement tool that taps into the collective wisdom and passion of the public, fostering a deep sense of involvement and ownership among contributors. By facilitating a platform where ideas, funds, and feedback flow freely from a diverse group of individuals, crowdsourcing has the potential to democ- ratize the preservation process, making it accessible to anyone with a connection to the site's heritage or a vested interest in its future.

Community Engagement

The essence of crowdsourcing in preservation lies in its ability to involve the community at every stage of the project. From the initial brainstorming of ideas to the final stages of restoration, every phase can benefit from the input and engagement of the crowd. Platforms like Kickstarter and GoFundMe have revolutionized the way funds are raised, allowing people from all over the world to contribute to projects that resonate with them personally. This model of fundraising not only gathers the necessary financial resources but also builds a community of supporters who feel personally invested in the success of the project. Beyond funding, crowdsourcing platforms can be used to gather historical information, personal stories, and creative ideas that enrich the understanding of the site's significance and inform more sensitive restoration plans. For example, a project aimed at restoring a historic marketplace might use crowdsourcing to collect old photographs, anecdotes from locals, and suggestions on how to best use the space in the future, thus ensuring the revitalized site remains true to its roots while serving current community needs.

Success Models

The success of crowdsourcing in historic preservation is exemplified by several standout projects that have harnessed the enthusiasm and resources of the public. One notable example is the restoration of a historic theater in a small town, where local residents used a crowdfunding campaign to raise the necessary funds. The campaign not only reached its financial goals but also sparked a renewed interest in the town's heritage, leading to further preservation initiatives. Another success story involves the restoration of an ancient fortress where crowdsourcing was used to involve global experts in medieval architecture. This collaborative approach raised funds and brought in international expertise, ensuring the restoration work was historically accurate and innovative. These models demonstrate how crowdsourcing can extend beyond financial contributions to include knowledge sharing and community building, ultimately leading to more successful and sustainable preservation outcomes.

Challenges and Opportunities

While crowdsourcing offers significant advantages, it also presents unique challenges that must be navigated carefully. One of the primary concerns is the reliability and consistency of funding. Unlike traditional funding sources, which typically provide large sums up front, crowdsourcing relies on the accumulation of many small contributions, which can be unpredictable and vary widely from project to project. Additionally, managing a large and diverse group of contributors can be complex, requiring transparent communication and robust management strategies to ensure everyone remains informed and engaged throughout the project. Despite these challenges, the opportunities presented by crowdsourcing for expanding public involvement and accessing diverse resources make it an invaluable tool in the preservation toolkit. By addressing these challenges with thoughtful strategies, preservation projects can leverage crowdsourcing to meet funding goals and foster a deeper connection with the community.

Best Practices

To maximize the benefits and minimize the challenges of crowdsourcing, several best practices should be followed. First, it is crucial to establish clear and transparent communication with contributors. Regular updates, detailed reports on the project's progress, and prompt responses to inquiries can help build trust and maintain engagement. Second, setting realistic goals and flexible plans allows for adjustments based on the funding and ideas received. This adaptability can be crucial for responding to the dynamic nature of crowdsourcing. Additionally, offering tangible rewards and recognition to contributors can enhance participation rates and encourage higher contributions. These rewards range from public ac- knowledgments and exclusive updates to invitations to special events once the project is completed.

In weaving together the threads of community engagement, success models, challenges, and best practices, crowdsourcing stands out as a revolutionary approach to historic preservation. It empowers individuals to play an active role in safeguarding the cultural heritage that resonates with them, transforming the traditional preservation landscape into a more democratic and participatory field. As more preservation projects adopt this approach, the potential for innovative solutions and broad-based support grows, promising a new era of preservation that is as inclusive as it is effective.

9.3 Predictive Analytics: Forecasting Success in Revitalization Projects

In the evolving landscape of town and historic revitalization, adopting predictive analytics heralds a shift towards more strategic and informed decision-making. At its core, predictive analytics uses historical data, statistical algorithms, and machine learning techniques to forecast future events. In the context of preservation and revitalization, this means having the capability to predict outcomes of various project scenarios, which can significantly enhance planning accuracy and project success. This approach streamlines project management and ensures that resources are allocated efficiently, risks are min- imized, and the anticipated benefits to the community and economy are maximized.

Data-Driven Decisions

The foundational element of predictive analytics in preservation projects is its focus on data-driven decisions. Predictive models can provide insights that guide current project planning by analyzing past projects, including successes and challenges. For instance, data on visitor numbers, community feedback, and economic impact from previous restoration projects can help predict the potential success of similar future endeavors. This method allows project managers to move beyond intuition and make decisions based on robust analytical evidence. Moreover, predictive analytics can identify trends and patterns that may not be immediately apparent through traditional analysis methods, offering a deeper understanding of the factors that influence project outcomes.

ToolsandTechniques

The tools and techniques used in predictive analytics are varied and can be highly sophisticated. At the basic level, data collection is paramount. This involves gathering quantitative data, such as cost and time metrics, as well as qualitative data, like stakeholder satisfaction and aesthetic value. Advanced statistical methods and machine learning algorithms are then applied to this data to model potential future outcomes. Software tools specializing in predictive analytics, such as SAS, SPSS, and R, provide platforms where data can be inputted and analyzed to generate predictive insights. Additionally, visualization tools like Tableau or Microsoft Power BI can transform complex data sets into understandable and actionable visual reports, making it easier for project teams to make informed decisions.

Improving Outcomes

The application of predictive analytics significantly enhances the likelihood of positive outcomes in revitalization projects. One of the primary benefits is the optimization of resource allocation. By predicting the resources required for different aspects of a project, managers can distribute budgets, staffing, and materials more effectively, reducing waste and increasing efficiency. Predictive analytics also plays a crucial role in risk management by forecasting potential challenges and allowing teams to develop mitigation strategies in advance. Furthermore, this approach can enhance visitor engagement and economic impact by predicting patterns in visitor behavior and spending. For instance, analytics can forecast peak visiting times, enabling better staffing and facility management to enhance visitor experience and maximize revenue.

Case Examples

The practical impact of predictive analytics is best illustrated through specific case examples where its application has led to measurable improvements in preservation projects. One notable example involves the restoration of a historic library where predictive analytics was used to forecast project costs and timelines based on data from similar previous projects. This predictive insight allowed the project team to optimize their workflow and resource allocation, completing the project ahead of schedule and under budget. Another example is the revitalization of a historic downtown area, where predictive models analyzed potential economic outcomes based on different development scenarios. This analysis helped the community and investors choose a development plan that maximized economic benefits while preserving the area's historic character.

As we reflect on the transformative potential of predictive analytics in town and historic revitalization, it becomes evident that this approach is not merely about forecasting the future— it's about creating it. By harnessing the power of data and advanced analytics, preservation projects can achieve not only greater efficiency and effectiveness but also foster deeper connections with the communities they serve. This chapter has explored the mechanisms through which predictive analytics can revolutionize preservation efforts, offering a glimpse into a future where every decision is informed, every risk is anticipated, and every outcome is optimized.

As we close this exploration of advanced technologies and methodologies reshaping the field of preservation, we look forward to the next chapter, which will delve into innovative funding strategies that can support these sophisticated projects. This upcoming discussion will highlight traditional funding avenues and explore new and emerging financial models that can ensure the sustainable success of preservation initiatives in the modern era.

Chapter 10: Urban Revitalization Strategies

As we navigate the evolving landscape of urban revitalization, our attention turns toward the pressing challenge of integrating high-density housing solutions within historic districts. This chapter delves into the delicate balance required to introduce modern living spaces into areas rich with historical significance, ensuring that our heritage's soul and fabric are preserved and enhanced. Here, you'll discover the art of blending contemporary architectural innovations with timeless historic elements, the critical role of regulatory frameworks, and the invaluable contribution of community involvement in shaping vibrant, livable urban spaces that respect the past while embracing the future.

10.1 High-Density Housing Solutions in Historic Districts

Innovative Design Approaches

In the quest to accommodate growing urban populations without sprawling into the green belts, high-density housing emerges as a crucial solution. However, when this solution is to be implemented in historic districts, it demands more than mere functionality—it requires creativity. Integrating high-density housing within these areas involves innovative architectural designs that complement the existing historical context. For instance, architects might employ façade treat- ments that echo the historic aesthetic, using materials and motifs that blend seamlessly with the old while introducing the benefits of modern construction technology. Techniques such as set- backs and step-backs are also employed to ensure that new structures do not overpower their historic neighbors in scale and sightlines. This thoughtful approach not only caters to the need for additional housing but also preserves the character and charm of historic districts, making them desirable places to live.

One innovative material that has gained popularity among con- servation architects is recycled brick. Not only does it maintain the visual continuity of historic neighborhoods, but it also adds an element of sustainability to new constructions. Similarly, modern lightweight glass structures can be designed to reflect the surroundings, thereby minimizing visual impact while providing the airy, bright interiors that contemporary residents seek. When used thoughtfully, these materials bridge the gap between old and new, ensuring that the district's historical essence is preserved while providing for contemporary needs.

Regulatory Frameworks

Successfully integrating high-density housing in historic districts relies on robust regulatory frameworks. These frameworks ensure that any development within historic precincts contributes positively to the area's cultural, aesthetic, and economic value. They involve detailed zoning laws, heritage preservation statutes, and building codes that specifically address the balance between new construction and historic preservation. For developers and architects, navigating these regulations can be as challenging as it is critical. The frameworks often require that new projects undergo rigorous review processes by heritage and urban planning boards, which as- sess the compatibility of new developments with the existing architectural and cultural context.

In cities like Charleston and Savannah, where historic districts are pivotal to their cultural identity, the local governments have established specific architectural review boards that work closely with developers to ensure that new constructions adhere to strict guidelines regarding height, density, and design aesthetics. These regulations protect the historic integrity while allowing for thoughtful modernization to accommodate a growing population and evolving urban needs.

Community Involvement

Every urban revitalization project can succeed with the heart and voice of its community. In historic districts, where the sense of place and identity is strong, community involvement becomes even more critical. Engaging local residents, business owners, and stakeholders in the planning process helps to ensure that the new developments meet both preservation standards and modern living needs. Public consultations, workshops, and participatory design processes effectively gather community input and foster a sense of ownership and accep- tance among the local population.

For instance, in a recent revitalization project in Boston's historic North End, the development team organized a series of community design workshops that allowed residents to voice their concerns, suggest ideas, and directly influence the design of new housing units. This collaborative approach not only smoothed the regulatory approval process but also ensured the project received broad community support, enhancing its success and sustainability.

Case Studies

Reflecting on successful case studies illuminates the path for- ward for integrating high-density housing in historic districts. A standout example is the revitalization of the Meatpacking District in New York City. Once a gritty industrial area, it has been transformed into a vibrant, mixed-use community that respects its architectural heritage. The introduction of high-density housing was carefully managed through stringent architectural controls and active community engagement. Another inspiring case is found in the historic district of Georgetown in Washington, D.C., where innovative zoning solutions have allowed for the development of multi-family dwellings that harmonize with the area's colonial architecture. These projects not only cater to the housing needs but also enhance the economic vitality of their districts, proving that with thoughtful planning and community cooperation, it is possible to meet the challenges of modern urban living without sacrificing historical charm.

As we explore these strategies and examples, it becomes clear that thoughtfully integrating high-density housing in historic districts is not just about creating more space—it's about weaving a new layer into the fabric of our communities that respects and revitalizes the old. This approach ensures that our historic districts remain monuments to our past and vibrant, living communities that continue to grow and thrive in the modern age.

10.2 Public Transit and Walkability: Enhancing Urban Livability

In the fabric of urban revitalization, integrating public transit solutions into historic urban areas offers a compelling narrative of progress and preservation. This approach not only caters to the modern necessity for efficient and accessible transportation but also respects the integrity of historic urban landscapes. Effective public transit systems, such as light rail, buses, and even modern tramways, can be designed to blend seamlessly with the historic character of urban areas. These systems reduce the reliance on personal vehicles, decrease traffic congestion, and lower pollution levels, thereby enhancing the overall quality of life in these culturally rich areas.

The key to successful integration lies in meticulous planning and design that considers the aesthetic and structural impacts on historic districts. For instance, tram lines can be embedded within existing roadways, and bus stops can be crafted with design elements that echo the architectural themes of the neighborhood. This careful consideration ensures that introducing modern transit solutions does not disrupt the historical charm but rather complements it. Moreover, the accessibility improvements brought by well-planned public transit systems make historic urban areas more inclusive. They allow people of all ages and abilities to enjoy these neighborhoods' rich heritage and amenities, thus enriching the urban experience for residents and visitors alike.

Improving walkability is another cornerstone of enhancing urban livability, particularly in areas with historic significance. The transformation of streets into pedestrian-friendly zones involves more than just the reduction of vehicular traffic; it encompasses a broader reimagining of public spaces. Sidewalks, for example, can be widened and enhanced with disability access, while historic cobblestone streets can be preserved and strengthened to accommodate both foot traffic and modern accessibility needs. Traffic calming measures, such as speed bumps, narrowed lanes, and pedestrian-only zones, not only make these areas safer for walkers but also encourage residents and tourists to engage more deeply with the local environment and economy.

The introduction of green corridors and pocket parks along these walkways can further enhance the pedestrian experience, offering scenic vistas and restful spots within bustling urban settings. These improvements make historic districts more navigable and enjoyable and foster a deeper connection between individuals and their surroundings, encouraging slower, more appreciative travel through areas rich with cultural and historical value.

The economic and social benefits of enhancing public transit and walkability in historic urban areas are profound and multifaceted. Economically, the increased accessibility and improved traffic conditions can lead to heightened commercial activity. Local businesses benefit from increased foot traffic, and property values often see an upward trend as the areas become more desirable. Socially, these enhancements contribute to public health by promoting walking and cycling, reducing vehicular emissions, and increasing social interaction, which enhances community cohesion and well-being.

Public spaces that are easily accessible and welcoming increase interactions among residents and foster a sense of community belonging. Moreover, beautifying these areas through thoughtful urban design can enhance collective civic pride, encouraging residents and businesses to invest further in their communities. The neighborhood's social fabric is strengthened as people feel more connected to their environment and each other, creating a vibrant urban life that draws a diverse group of people and activities.

Turning to success stories, cities worldwide have demonstrated that integrating public transit and enhanced walkability can profoundly transform historic urban areas. Consider the example of Freiburg, Germany, renowned for its sustainable urban planning. The city's extensive tram system and pedestrian zones have revitalized its medieval center, making it one of the most livable urban areas in Europe. Similarly, in the United States, Portland, Oregon, has successfully integrated a modern light rail system with protected bike lanes and pedestrian pathways, revitalizing its historic downtown and contributing to the city's reputation as a sustainable urban hub.

These examples underscore the transformative power of well-integrated public transit systems and walkability enhancements in maintaining urban areas' historical integrity and vitality. By prioritizing accessibility and community engagement, cities can ensure that their historic districts do not just survive but thrive amidst the challenges and opportunities of the 21st century. As we continue to explore the dynamics of urban revitalization, these principles serve as a beacon for other cities aiming to balance heritage preservation with modern urban needs.

10.3 Vertical Gardens and Green Spaces in Urban Preservation

In the heart of our bustling cities, where historic charm meets urban hustle, the integration of vertical gardens and green spaces brings a breath of fresh air. These innovative green solutions not only enhance the aesthetic appeal of historic urban districts but also play a crucial role in improving air quality and overall environmental health. Incorporating such spaces is not just about adding splashes of green; it's about rethinking urban landscapes to create sustainable, livable environments that respect and enhance our historical heritage.

Vertical gardens, also known as living walls, are particularly suited to historic districts where ground space for traditional gardens is often scarce. These green installations can transform bare walls and unused vertical spaces into lush, vibrant features. Not only do they increase the green area without encroaching on valuable ground space, but they also add a layer of thermal insulation to buildings, helping to regulate indoor temperatures naturally. The aesthetic transformation brought about by these gardens can turn historical buildings into landmarks of modern sustainability, making them points of interest that draw both locals and tourists. The choice of plants is crucial; species that are native to the area or are particularly effective at air purification can be prioritized to maximize the environmental benefits.

In addition to their visual and environmental appeal, vertical gardens contribute significantly to the sustainability of urban historic districts through stormwater management. These living walls can absorb and filter rainwater, which reduces runoff and decreases the burden on urban drainage systems. This capability is particularly important in historic areas where outdated infrastructure may be overwhelmed by heavy rains. Furthermore, by mitigating the urban heat island effect, where built-up areas are significantly warmer than their rural surroundings, vertical gardens help maintain a more stable and comfortable urban microclimate. This cooling effect makes the urban environment more pleasant for residents and visitors, encouraging longer stays and increased interaction with the historic setting.

Community engagement is pivotal in the design and maintenance of these green spaces. Involving local residents and stakeholders in the planning process ensures that the green interventions meet the aesthetic and functional needs of the community. Workshops and participatory design sessions can be organized to gather input and foster a sense of ownership among the community members. Moreover, maintenance, which is crucial for the success of vertical gardens and green spaces, can become a community activity. Volunteer groups can be formed to care for these spaces, turning maintenance into an opportunity for community building and education on sustainability practices.

Innovative examples of these concepts abound. In Paris, the Musée du Quai Branly features a stunning vertical garden that wraps around the building, blending art, culture, and sustainability. This installation enhances the museum's exterior and contributes to the museum's environmental control system, showcasing how functional and aesthetic goals can be aligned. Another example is found in the historic district of Brera in Milan, where ancient buildings sport vertical gardens that both beautify the area and help reduce the city's overall carbon footprint. These examples demonstrate the versatility and adaptability of green spaces in enhancing urban livability and sustainability within historic precincts.

As we integrate these green innovations into our historic districts, we not only breathe new life into these areas but also set a precedent for sustainable urban living that respects our past while building toward a future. These green spaces act as bridges, connecting the historical significance of urban districts with modern ecological consciousness, creating a harmonious blend of old and new.

As this chapter concludes, it's clear that the strategies discussed here are more than mere enhancements; they are essential components of a holistic approach to urban revitalization. By incorporating vertical gardens and innovative green spaces, historic urban districts can transform into vibrant, sustainable environments that honor their past while looking forward to a greener future. This exploration sets the stage for the next chapter, where we will delve into the innovative funding strategies that can support these green initiatives, ensuring that our historic districts survive and thrive in an era of urban transformation.

Chapter 11: Suburban and Rural Revitalization Techniques

Imagine strolling down a vibrant Main Street, where each storefront is bustling with activity, the air vibrates with the buzz of community interactions, and historic charm is palpably woven through the modern hustle. This vision is at the heart of revitalizing small towns, where Main Streets serve as economic hubs and as the lifeblood of community identity and heritage. In this chapter, we delve into the transformative strategies that can reignite these essential urban arteries' economic, cultural, and social vitality.

11.1 Reviving Main Streets: Strategies for Small Towns

Economic Development Initiatives

At the core of revitalizing Main Streets is the thrust of economic development initiatives tailored to breathe new life into small towns. Supporting local businesses and nurturing entrepreneurship are pivotal strategies in this revitalization saga. Initiatives such as providing startup grants, facilitating low-interest loans, and offering tax incentives are crucial in attracting and retaining businesses that contribute to the economic fabric of the town. Moreover, programs like 'shop local' campaigns can foster a community-focused consumer base that supports local merchants and craftspeople. These efforts collectively create a sustainable economic environment that boosts local commerce and reinforces the town's uniqueness and appeal.

Another dynamic aspect of economic revitalization includes the development of incubation centers for small businesses. These centers offer crucial resources such as shared spaces, technology access, and professional guidance, lowering the barriers for new entrepreneurs and fostering a collaborative business community. Such initiatives not only help cultivate a culture of innovation and entrepreneurship but also weave a tight-knit network of local businesses that drive economic growth and job creation.

Cultural and Social Programming

Beyond economics, the cultural and social revitalization of Main Streets plays a significant role in rekindling the community spirit and enhancing the quality of life for residents and visitors alike. Integrating cultural and social programming involves hosting community-driven events such as festivals, art shows, farmers' markets, and holiday celebrations that spotlight local traditions and crafts. These events serve as both a celebration of local heritage and a catalyst for economic activity, drawing visitors from beyond the local community and providing markets for local artisans and producers.

Programming that leverages the town's unique history and culture can transform Main Streets into vibrant showcases of community pride and creativity. For example, historical reenactments, heritage walks, museum nights, entertainment, and education deepen communal ties to the town's history, attracting tourism and fostering a sense of belonging among residents.

Infrastructure Improvements

Revitalizing Main Streets also demands attention to infrastructure enhancements that make these spaces more accessible, safe, and attractive. Improvements such as pedestrian-friendly sidewalks, adequate street lighting, and well-maintained public areas are fundamental. Moreover, the aesthetic enhancement of these spaces through the preservation of historical architecture, the installation of public art, and the beautification of street landscapes can significantly elevate the visitor experience and enhance local pride.

Investing in 'smart' infrastructure can further enhance the functionality and appeal of Main Streets. Features like free public Wi-Fi, electric vehicle charging stations, and interactive informational kiosks can modernize historic thoroughfares, making them more navigable and aligned with contemporary urban needs.

Successful Revitalization Examples

Reflecting on successful examples provides tangible insights into the effective revitalization of Main Streets. Consider the transformation of Main Street in Greenville, South Carolina. Through a combination of public and private investments, Greenville transformed its once-dilapidated Main Street into a bustling avenue lined with local businesses, green spaces, and art installations. The city's strategy included widening sidewalks, adding bike lanes, and fostering a vibrant arts scene, which together helped in attracting both new businesses and tourists.

Another exemplary case is the revitalization of Main Street in Baker City, Oregon. Through comprehensive planning that included infrastructure improvements, cultural programming, and economic incentives, Baker City rejuvenated its historic Main Street into a dynamic hub of commerce and culture. The town now hosts numerous events throughout the year that celebrate its rich heritage and attract visitors from across the region, contributing significantly to its economy.

In weaving together these strategies and examples, we see a tapestry of potential for small towns aiming to revitalize their Main Streets. By fostering economic growth, celebrating cultural identity, enhancing infrastructure, and learning from successful revitalizations, these towns can ensure that their Main Streets flourish as vibrant, attractive, and economically sustainable spaces. Let's carry forward this spirit of renewal and innovation as we explore the preservation of agricultural heritage in the next segment, ensuring that our suburban and rural landscapes thrive in harmony with their historic roots and contemporary advancements.

11.2 Agricultural Heritage: Preserving Rural Landscapes and Traditions

Imagine the rolling fields of rural landscapes, where the heritage of farming communities is embedded in every furrow and fence line. In these bastions of tradition, it's here that the preservation of agricultural land and rural culture holds the key to sustainable development and cultural continuity. As urban expansion and industrial farming threaten these areas, strategic measures to protect and valorize rural and agricultural heritage are essential. Conservation easements, heritage designations, and promoting sustainable farming practices emerge as vital tools in this endeavor, ensuring that these landscapes continue to sustain and inspire future generations.

Preservation of Agricultural Land

Preserving agricultural land involves more than halting urban sprawl; it's about recognizing the intrinsic value of these landscapes as reservoirs of biodiversity, history, and traditional farming practices. Strategies such as conservation easements— a tool that allows landowners to restrict the type of activities on their land—have proven effective. These legal agreements ensure that the land is preserved for agricultural use and pro- tected from development that could alter its character. Heritage designation is another powerful strategy, where significant landscapes are recognized for their cultural and historical importance, granting them protection and often financial support for conservation. These designations help maintain the scenic beauty and ecological health of rural areas, supporting them against the pressures of modernization and neglect.

Furthermore, agricultural land trusts play a pivotal role in this preservation effort. By acquiring development rights through purchases or donations, these trusts can protect large swaths of agricultural land from being converted into non-agricultural uses. This not only preserves the landscape but also supports local food systems and maintains the economic viability of rural communities. The benefits extend beyond the borders of the farms, contributing to regional environmental health, including watershed protection and carbon sequestration, thus intertwining agricultural preservation with broader ecological goals.

Sustainable Farming Practices

Transitioning to sustainable farming practices is fundamental to the longevity of rural areas. These practices, which include crop rotation, organic farming, and the use of renewable resources, not only improve soil health and productivity but also reduce dependency on chemical inputs, enhancing the overall resilience of farms to climate change and market fluctuations. Agroforestry, the integration of trees and shrubs into agricultural landscapes, exemplifies a sustainable practice that benefits both farmers and the environment. This method increases biodiversity, improves soil structure, and provides additional income sources such as timber or fruit, all while maintaining the scenic value of the landscape.

Community-supported agriculture (CSA) programs also embody sustainable practices by fostering direct relationships between farmers and consumers. These programs encourage local consumption and support sustainable farming by providing farmers with a guaranteed market for their produce. Consumers benefit from fresh, locally-grown food, and farmers receive a stable income stream, reducing the economic pressures that might otherwise lead them to adopt more intensive, less sustainable farming methods.

Cultural Preservation

Rural traditions and cultural heritage are inextricably linked to the identity of agricultural communities. Preserving these traditions involves more than just maintaining landscapes; it's about keeping the community fabric intact and vibrant. Initiatives like community storytelling, where the histories and anecdotes of older generations are recorded and celebrated, help keep the cultural heritage alive. Local festivals and agricultural fairs, where traditional crafts and farming techniques are showcased, play a crucial role in this respect. These events serve as both an education in rural life for the wider public and a celebration of the community's enduring connection to the land.

Preserving traditional farming methods, often more sustainable and adapted to local environmental conditions, also contributes to cultural preservation. These methods passed down through generations, embody a deep understanding of the land and its capacities, representing a cumulative knowledge base that is invaluable for sustainable development.

Case Studies in Rural Revitalization

Examining case studies where agricultural preservation has been successfully integrated with economic and cultural revitalization provides actionable insights. In the Tuscany region of Italy, for example, the combination of agricultural land trusts, heritage designations, and the promotion of agrotourism has not only preserved the iconic Tuscan landscape but also bolstered the local economy. Tourists are drawn to the area for its beauty and the opportunity to experience traditional Italian farm life, providing farmers with an alternative source of income through farm stays, wine tastings, and culinary tours.

Another example is found in Shikoku Island in Japan, where the preservation of terraced rice fields has played a central role in the area's cultural revival. These fields are not only productive agricultural assets but also a part of the region's cultural heritage, attracting visitors and sustaining local traditions. The community has established a museum dedicated to the history and technique of terrace farming, and locals conduct workshops and tours that educate visitors on sustainable farming practices and the importance of preserving rural landscapes.

In weaving together these strategies and examples, the chapter underscores the multifaceted approach needed to successfully preserve rural landscapes and traditions. By fostering sustainable practices, protecting agricultural land, and celebrating rural culture, communities can ensure that their heritage is preserved, cherished, and sustained in the face of modern challenges. This holistic approach to rural revitalization maintains the ecological and aesthetic values of these landscapes and supports the social and economic fabric of the communities that depend on them.

11.3 Enhancing Connectivity: Bridging the Urban-Rural Divide

When you consider the vast expanse that separates bustling urban centers from tranquil rural areas, the significance of robust connectivity becomes undeniably clear. Improving transportation links is not just about facilitating easier commutes; it's about weaving a tighter economic and social integration fabric that benefits everyone. Enhanced transportation networks allow people to live in serene rural or suburban areas while working in vibrant urban centers, thereby distributing economic opportunities more evenly and alleviating urban congestion and housing pressures.

Investing in transportation infrastructure—such as roads, bridges, and public transit systems—can dramatically reduce the isolation of rural areas. Improved road systems decrease travel times and costs, making it feasible for businesses to operate in and around these regions and for residents to access services and employment opportunities in urban areas. Public transit options like regional bus services or rail links further enhance this connectivity, providing reliable and affordable alternatives to personal vehicles, which might be beyond the reach of many rural households. Additionally, these transit solutions contribute significantly to reducing carbon footprints, aligning with broader environmental sustainability goals.

But physical connectivity is just one piece of the puzzle. In today's digital age, the role of comprehensive digital infrastructure cannot be overstated. Broadband internet is as crucial as any utility service, perhaps even more so in the wake of the global shift toward remote work. For rural communities, robust digital connectivity ensures that residents and businesses can participate fully in the digital economy. This includes everything from accessing e-government services and telehealth to engaging in e-commerce and remote learning. Initiatives to expand broadband access in these areas, coupled with the establishment of remote working hubs, can transform rural towns into attractive living and working destinations, thus revitalizing these communities.

Collaborative regional planning is essential to ensure that enhancements in connectivity deliver widespread benefits. This approach involves multiple stakeholders—including government entities, business leaders, community groups, and policymakers—working together to develop strategies that align with both regional and local needs. Effective collaboration ensures that infrastructure improvements are well-planned and sustainable, reflecting the shared goals of various commu- nities. For instance, when urban and rural areas collaborate on transport planning, they can create systems that boost economic development while preserving the rural lifestyle, which many residents cherish.

Examples of Enhanced Connectivity

Examining regions that have successfully enhanced their connectivity offers valuable lessons. One notable example is the Chattanooga, Tennessee area, which has leveraged its status as one of the first cities in the U.S. to offer a citywide gigabit internet service. This technological advancement has attracted many tech companies and startups, transforming the city into a tech hub and providing immense economic benefits to the surrounding rural areas. Similarly, introducing high-speed rail links between major cities and their surrounding countryside in parts of Europe has allowed smaller towns and rural areas to thrive, preventing the urban drain often seen when residents flock to larger cities for better opportunities.

In another instance, regions like the Silicon Valley have implemented regional bike share programs and expanded public transit routes that not only improve access to the urban core but also enhance connectivity between suburban and rural areas. These efforts facilitate easier commutes for residents living outside the urban sprawl, allowing them to participate fully in the economic and social life of the bustling tech hub.

Through these examples, it becomes evident that when regions invest wisely in both physical and digital connectivity, the benefits extend across the urban-rural spectrum, fostering more integrated and resilient communities. This strategic approach bridges the physical distance and narrows the opportunity gap between urban and rural areas, setting a foundation for sustained economic growth and enhanced social cohesion across diverse landscapes.

As this chapter closes, reflecting on integrating enhanced connectivity within suburban and rural revitalization strategies highlights a crucial pathway toward more balanced regional development. By fostering both traditional and digital connectivity, these areas can attract new residents, support local businesses, and participate more fully in the broader economy. This discussion sets the stage for the subsequent exploration of innovative funding strategies that can support these vital connectivity initiatives, ensuring that the benefits of revitalization are both far-reaching and sustainable.

Chapter 12: Special Considerations for Coastal and Historic Waterfront Communities

Imagine standing on the weathered docks of a historic coastal town, where the ocean air mingles with centuries of history. With their unique cultural and historical landscapes, these waterfront communities face unprecedented challenges in the face of climate change. Rising sea levels, increasingly unpredictable weather patterns, and the relentless force of erosion pose significant threats. Yet, these communities are not passive witnesses to change; they are active participants in crafting innovative, sustainable solutions that safeguard their heritage and secure their future.

12.1 Sea-Level Rise and Climate Resilience in Historic Coastal Towns

Climate Adaptation Strategies

For historic coastal towns, the rising sea levels aren't just a forecast; they're an evolving reality that demands immediate and strategic responses. Adaptation strategies such as constructing robust flood defenses and integrating resilient infrastructure form the first line of defense against the encroaching seas. Consider the innovation behind the floating barriers used in Venice, a city synonymous with both water and historical significance. These barriers, designed to rise with the tide, demonstrate the harmony between modern engineering and historic preservation, protecting the city's irreplaceable architecture from flooding without compromising its charm or historical integrity.

Beyond physical barriers, the adaptation strategies extend to comprehensive urban planning, incorporating climate resilience into every facet of community development. Zoning laws, for example, are recalibrated to restrict new construction in areas most vulnerable to sea-level rise, while building codes are enhanced to require that structures not only withstand floods but also provide safe havens during extreme weather events. Green infrastructure plays a pivotal role here, integrating rain gardens, permeable pavements, and restored wetlands to naturally mitigate flood risks while enhancing the urban landscape.

Preservation Under Threat

The relentless advance of climate change poses a nuanced threat to the architectural heritage of coastal towns. Saltwater intrusion and heightened humidity can accelerate the deterioration of ancient building materials, leading to a loss of structural integrity and historical detail. The challenge here is to devise preservation techniques that respect the original materials and construction methods while enhancing resilience. One promising approach involves the use of modern materials that mimic the aesthetic and functional properties of traditional ones but offer greater resistance to environmental stressors. For example, new forms of lime-based mortar and plasters that can withstand higher moisture levels without degrading are being developed.

Simultaneously, there's a growing reliance on technology to monitor and predict the impacts of climate change on these historic sites. High-resolution imaging and 3D modeling allow preservationists to anticipate areas of potential damage and intervene proactively. These technologies not only help in planning restoration projects more effectively but also in documenting and archiving the minutiae of architectural heritage for future generations.

Community Engagement in Resilience Planning

The fabric of any successful adaptation strategy is woven with the threads of community involvement. Engaging local residents, business owners, and stakeholders in resilience planning ensures that the solutions developed are comprehensive and embraced by those they are meant to protect. Community workshops, public consultations, and participatory planning sessions become vital platforms for dialogue, where local knowledge and historical perspectives merge with expert insights to forge robust resilience strategies.

In these forums, the community's attachment to their heritage sites and firsthand experiences of climate impacts provide invaluable context for the adaptation measures. Moreover, these interactions foster a sense of shared responsibility and collective action, which is essential for any resilience initiative's sustained success.

Case Studies in Climate Resilience

Looking at how various coastal towns have turned the tide on climate challenges offers both inspiration and practical blueprints for others. For instance, in Charleston, South Carolina, the city's long-term resilience initiative has successfully integrated strict building codes with extensive community outreach programs, creating a model of enhancing urban resilience without sacrificing historical integrity. Another example is the small town of Hoi An in Vietnam, where a combination of community-led mangrove restoration projects and elevated pathways has not only reduced flood risk but also boosted tourism, turning ecological resilience into an economic boon.

In Newfoundland, Canada, the community's response to sea- level rise has been both proactive and innovative. By relocating some historical buildings to higher ground, the town has preserved its cultural heritage while adapting to the new climate realities. This approach, while drastic, highlights the lengths to which communities are willing to go to safeguard their history.

Each of these cases underscores the intricate dance between preserving the past and preparing for the future, a dynamic that coastal towns worldwide are mastering with creativity and courage. As we continue to explore the unique challenges faced by coastal and historic waterfront communities, the lessons gleaned from these pioneers in climate resilience illuminate a path forward for survival and thriving in an uncertain future.

12.2 Revitalizing Historic Waterfronts: Balancing Commerce and Preservation

When you consider the unique charm and historical significance of waterfronts, their potential as catalysts for urban revitalization becomes evident. Waterfronts often serve as the face of coastal towns, showcasing a blend of cultural heritage and natural beauty. However, developing these areas in a way that stimulates economic growth while preserving their historical essence requires a nuanced approach. Strategies for waterfront development must carefully balance new commercial opportunities with conserving the area's historical identity. This involves integrating modern urban design with traditional architecture, ensuring new developments complement rather than overshadow the historic character of the waterfront.

One effective strategy is the adaptive reuse of old waterfront buildings. By transforming historic warehouses, docks, and marketplaces into mixed-use developments that house shops, restaurants, and cultural spaces, cities can breathe new life into these areas while maintaining their historical integrity. This approach not only preserves the architectural heritage but also creates vibrant, multifunctional spaces that attract both locals and tourists. The key here is sensitivity to the original architectural styles and urban fabric, which can be maintained through careful design guidelines and thoughtful planning processes.

Furthermore, the introduction of sustainable infrastructure is crucial in modernizing historic waterfronts without compromising their environmental or aesthetic values. Green building practices, such as the use of eco-friendly materials and energy-efficient systems, contribute to the sustainability of waterfront developments. Additionally, the integration of natural elements, like coastal gardens and porous surfaces, can enhance the resilience of these areas to environmental stresses, including rising sea levels and increased storm surges, while also improving the overall attractiveness of the waterfront.

Economic Revitalization

Historic waterfronts hold immense potential for economic revitalization, particularly through the development of tourism, maritime industries, and waterfront businesses. By leveraging their unique location and historical appeal, these areas can transform into economic powerhouses that provide substantial revenue and employment opportunities. Tourism, in particular, plays a pivotal role in this regard. The aesthetic and historical allure of well-preserved waterfronts draws visitors from around the globe, eager to experience the blend of history and natural beauty. To capitalize on this, towns can develop thematic tours, maritime museums, and cultural festivals that celebrate their historical and maritime heritage.

Moreover, the revitalization of waterfronts often leads to the resurgence of maritime industries. Traditional crafts such as boat building, sail making, and marine repair can be revitalized and marketed not only as functional businesses but also as living museums, offering demonstrations and workshops that attract tourists and provide educational content. Additionally, modern maritime activities like marinas, fishing charters, and eco-tours can create new business opportunities that align with the sustainable use of waterfront resources.

Waterfront businesses, including restaurants, cafes, and retail stores, benefit significantly from the increased foot traffic that a vibrant, historical waterfront attracts. These businesses contribute to the economic sustainability of the area, creating jobs and generating tax revenue. The key is building a business environment that supports both new ventures and traditional businesses, ensuring a dynamic yet cohesive economic land- scape.

Public Access and Recreation

Improving public access and recreational opportunities is fundamental to revitalizing historic waterfronts. When these areas are accessible and welcoming, they become cherished parts of the urban landscape, enhancing community well-being and enriching the visitor experience. Strategies to improve access include developing walkable waterfront esplanades, cycling paths, and public piers that allow people to engage directly with the water. These pathways not only make the waterfront more accessible but also encourage physical activity and provide spaces for social interaction, which are essential for a healthy urban life.

In addition to access, recreational opportunities such as open-air theaters, water-based activities, and public art installations can animate historic waterfronts, making them more attractive to residents and tourists. These activities should be designed to reflect the waterfront's cultural and historical significance, creating a recreational experience that is both enjoyable and educational. For instance, kayak tours along a historic canal can offer insights into the area's industrial heritage while providing an engaging recreational activity.

Successful Waterfront Revitalization Projects

Reflecting on successful waterfront revitalization projects offers valuable insights into practical strategies and outcomes. The transformation of the Baltimore Inner Harbor from an industrial wasteland into a thriving public space is a prime example. The project involved the conversion of old warehouses into shops and restaurants, the establishment of a renowned aquarium, and the development of ample public spaces that encouraged community activities and events. This revitalization boosted Baltimore's economy through tourism and business growth and reconnected the city with its waterfront heritage, making the harbor a focal point of city life.

Another notable example is the redevelopment of the Liverpool Waterfront in the United Kingdom, which cleverly combined the preservation of its iconic historical buildings, like the Royal Liver Building, with the introduction of new cultural institutions, such as the Museum of Liverpool and the Tate Liverpool art gallery. This approach not only preserved the architectural heritage of the waterfront but also established Liverpool as a cultural hub, significantly enhancing its appeal to visitors and locals alike.

These examples underscore the transformative impact that thoughtful waterfront revitalization can have on a community's economic and social fabric. They prove that with the right balance of preservation and development, historic waterfronts can thrive as vibrant, economically robust, and culturally rich spaces.

12.3 Maritime Heritage: Preserving and Celebrating Coastal Cultures

Maritime heritage holds a treasure trove of stories, traditions, and historical artifacts that are pivotal in understanding coastal communities' cultural and historical landscape. Preserving these elements, from historic ships and port buildings to maritime artifacts, is not just about maintaining physical objects; it's about keeping the narratives that define the identity of coastal populations alive. Effective conservation methods are multifaceted, involving both physical preservation techniques and the integration of modern technologies to document and protect maritime heritage against the ravages of time and environmental threats.

For instance, preserving historic ships often involves dry docking where necessary repairs and restorations can be made while allowing the public to view and learn about the craftsmanship and history of these vessels. Techniques such as 3D scanning and digital modeling offer ways to capture detailed information about the ships, which can be used for educational purposes and virtual tours, thus broadening access and engagement. Additionally, the treatment of maritime artifacts requires specialized conservation techniques that prevent degradation from salt and moisture, which are common in marine environments. Here, the use of desalination treatments and controlled atmospheres can play a crucial role in extending the life of these valuable pieces of history.

Beyond the physical preservation, the role of cultural programming in maritime heritage conservation is equally significant. Festivals, museums, and educational programs not only celebrate this rich heritage but also play a crucial part in revitalizing coastal communities. Maritime festivals, for example, can transform local economies by attracting tourism and stimulating local businesses. These events provide a platform for artisans, performers, and educators to showcase maritime skills, crafts, and history, bringing the community together to celebrate their shared heritage. Museums dedicated to maritime history serve as custodians of the past, housing artifacts and narratives that might otherwise be lost. Through interactive exhibits and educational programs, they engage visitors and locals alike, fostering a deeper appreciation and understanding of the maritime past and its impact on present-day life.

Community involvement is paramount in these efforts. When local residents participate in preserving and celebrating their maritime heritage, they keep their history alive and strengthen their cultural identity and community bonds. Initiatives like volunteer programs for ship restoration or docent training in museums can empower individuals to take active roles in their heritage. This participation enhances individual and collective pride and ensures that the knowledge and skills associated with maritime traditions are passed on to future generations.

Several coastal communities stand out in terms of successful preservation and promotion of maritime heritage. In the small town of Mystic, Connecticut, the Mystic Seaport Museum offers a blend of preservation and education. It operates a working shipyard, where traditional techniques are used to restore historic vessels, and provides a range of programming that immerses visitors in maritime history. Another example is in Norway, where the coastal community of Alesund revitalized its economy and cultural scene by restoring its old waterfront and converting part of it into a museum dedicated to the local fishing industry, including boat-building workshops and seafood preparation classes.

These examples highlight the dynamic ways in which maritime heritage can be leveraged not only to preserve the past but also to enrich the future. By integrating conservation efforts with vibrant cultural programming and active community participation, coastal towns can ensure that their maritime heritage remains a living, thriving part of their cultural landscape.

As this exploration of maritime heritage concludes, the impor- tance of these efforts resonates more than ever. By preserving the vessels, buildings, and traditions of our coastal forebears, we keep alive a vital part of our cultural fabric. This chapter has woven through various strategies and real-world applications, highlighting how maritime preservation can be effectively achieved while enhancing community life and tourism. The subsequent chapter will delve into innovative methods for funding these vital initiatives, ensuring that the heritage that has survived centuries can continue to be a beacon of cultural pride and historical education for future generations.

Chapter 13: Demystifying Historic Preservation

Imagine you are walking through the heart of a bustling city, where modern skyscrapers tower above, yet nestled among these giants are the quiet custodians of history— buildings that have stood the test of time. It's here, in the juxtaposition of old and new, that we confront the myths surrounding historic preservation. Often seen as a luxury or an economically burdensome endeavor, historic preservation is, in fact, an investment in our cultural legacy and a catalyst for economic vitality. This chapter aims to shed light on the true costs and benefits of preserving our architectural heritage, debunking prevailing myths, and revealing the untold advantages of such endeavors.

13.1 Busting Myths: The True Costs and Benefits of Preservation

Clarifying Preservation Costs

The notion that historic preservation is prohibitively expensive pervades public perception, yet a closer examination reveals a different narrative. Comparatively, the costs of demolition and new construction are often higher than those of preservation. New construction involves significant expenditure on materials, labor, and, critically, the environmental costs of new material production and waste. In contrast, preservation maxi- mizes the use of existing materials and structures, significantly reducing the need for new resources and minimizing waste generation. The preservation of buildings also often qualifies for various tax incentives, grants, and funding opportunities not available for new construction, aiding in the financial feasibility of such projects.

For example, the renovation of the historic Paramount Theater in Austin, Texas, showed that updating and preserving the site was 40% less expensive than demolishing it and building a new structure in its place. This cost efficiency comes from utilizing the existing structure and materials, which often only need refurbishment or minor updates to meet modern standards. This preservation aspect allows for a more resource-efficient approach to urban development, which saves money and con- serves the craftsmanship and materials often irreplaceable in today's market.

Highlighting Economic Benefits

Beyond the immediate financial savings, historic preservation acts as a catalyst for broader economic benefits. Preserved historic sites are significant draws for tourism, a major industry in many local economies. Tourists are often attracted to unique historical sites that offer a glimpse into the past, thereby boosting local businesses, including hotels, restaurants, and retail shops.

Moreover, historic preservation supports local economies through job creation. Preservation-focused projects typically require specialized skills such as stonemasonry, carpentry, and traditional glasswork. These labor-intensive jobs are locally sourced, thus keeping the economic benefits within thecommunity. For instance, studies have shown that preservation projects can create 50% more jobs than the same amount of investment in new construction.

Environmental Advantages

The environmental benefits of historic preservation are profound yet frequently overlooked. Preservation reduces the demand for new materials, decreasing energy consumption and carbon emissions associated with manufacturing and transporting these materials. Additionally, by retaining the original structures, preservation significantly reduces the volume of debris sent to landfills compared to demolition. Buildings themselves are significant stores of carbon, and demolishing them releases this stored carbon back into the atmosphere.

Social and Cultural Gains

Preserving historic buildings enriches community identity and heritage, offering a tangible connection to the past that newer structures often fail to provide. These buildings become focal points for storytelling, education, and cultural activities that strengthen community ties and foster a sense of pride and belonging.

Moreover, historic districts often serve as excellent examples of human-scaled, walkable communities that modern urban planning seeks to replicate. These areas enhance social interaction and accessibility, creating more vibrant and cohesive communities. For example, the Gaslamp Quarter in San Diego, California, once slated for demolition, was preserved and is now a thriving hub of social and cultural activity, illustrating how historic areas can become lively parts of the urban fabric.

Through detailed exploration and myth-busting, this chapter reveals that historic preservation is not merely a nostalgic endeavor but a strategic approach that offers substantial economic, environmental, and social benefits. By shifting perspectives from viewing preservation as a cost to recognizing it as an investment, communities can unlock the full potential of their historical assets, ensuring these structures continue to enrich our landscapes and lives for generations to come.

13.2 Historic Sites Are Not Frozen in Time: Dynamic Uses and Adaptations

Historic sites often evoke images of static museums where time stands still, encapsulating a moment from the distant past. However, the reality is far more dynamic, with many of these sites undergoing thoughtful adaptations to serve contemporary societal needs while preserving their historical essence. Adaptive reuse, a key strategy in this process, involves repurposing old buildings for new uses, allowing them to remain vibrant and functional within modern communities. This approach conserves resources and provides these structures with a new lease on life, ensuring their sustainability and relevance in today's world.

Adaptive reuse projects vary widely, ranging from converting old mills into residential apartments or transforming abandoned railway stations into bustling retail spaces. Each project carries its own set of challenges and opportunities, but the successful ones find a balance where modern functionality meets historical integrity. For instance, an old factory may discover a new purpose as a tech hub, integrating cutting-edge infrastructure while retaining original architectural features like brick walls and large windows. These projects often become celebrated examples of how the past can be woven into the fabric of contemporary urban life, providing unique, character- rich spaces that stand out in a world often dominated by generic construction.

One notable example of adaptive reuse is a former brewery

that has turned into a community arts center. Here, the vast spaces once used for brewing and storage now host art galleries, studios, and performance venues. The renovation carefully preserved the industrial aesthetic, including maintaining the old copper vats and exposed beams, which now contribute to the artistic atmosphere of the space. This transformation not only saved the building from potential demolition but also turned it into a cultural hub that draws visitors and locals alike, fostering a vibrant community around the arts.

Moreover, the concept of modern functionality extends beyond mere structural adaptations. It encompasses integrating contemporary standards such as accessibility and sustainability into historic sites. Ensuring accessibility involves installing features like ramps and elevators that do not detract from the building's historic character. Sustainability initiatives might include updating the HVAC systems to more energy- efficient models or installing solar panels in a way that does not compromise the site's visual or architectural integrity. These enhancements make historic sites more inclusive and environmentally responsible, aligning them with present-day values and regulations.

Turning historic sites into community centers is another profound way these treasures continue to serve the public. By hosting events, workshops, and meetings, these sites become places where the past and present community life intertwines. An old mansion turned into a community center can provide a picturesque backdrop for social events and educational pro- grams, making history a part of everyday life. These centers often become the heartbeat of their neighborhoods, places where people gather, learn, and celebrate together, strengthening community bonds and fostering a deeper appreciation for the local heritage.

Innovation in preservation is crucial for adapting historic sites to contemporary uses. It requires creative thinking and a willingness to embrace change while respecting the past. This might involve using cutting-edge technology to create augmented reality tours that bring historic tales to life or employing modern art installations that highlight and contrast with the ancient features of a site. Such innovations attract a broader audience and create multi-layered experiences that enrich visitors' understanding and appreciation of history.

Each successful project serves as a testament to the versatility and enduring relevance of historic sites. Through adaptive reuse, these places can continue to contribute to their communities, providing spaces that reflect our past and are fully engaged with the present and future. As society continues to evolve, so too will the roles of these historic sites, adapting to meet new needs and continuing to remind us where we came from, all while contributing to where we are going.

13.3 Preservation and Modern Urban Needs: A Harmonious Relationship

In the evolving landscape of urban development, integrating historic preservation with modern needs often needs to be more manageable. Yet, when navigated with care and strategic planning, this integration becomes feasible and mutually beneficial, enhancing both the historical richness and the contemporary vitality of urban spaces. Practical strategies to balance these seemingly competing interests are crucial in ensuring cities retain their unique character while advancing toward modern functionality and sustainability.

A critical component of this balancing act involves zoning and planning policies that recognize the value of historic struc- tures. By implementing policies that encourage the retention and adaptive reuse of historic buildings within development projects, cities can maintain historical integrity while accommodating new business and residential needs. For instance, certain zoning allowances, such as height bonuses or floor area ratios, can be adjusted to incentivize developers to preserve and incorporate historic elements into their projects. This approach protects the architectural heritage and ensures that it remains a living part of the urban landscape, adapting to contemporary uses.

Urban design guidelines can also significantly contribute to harmonizing old and new structures. These guidelines can dictate elements like building scale, materials, and facade treatments to ensure that new developments complement the historical context. By requiring that new constructions respect the visual and architectural language of historical neighborhoods, these guidelines help maintain a cohesive urban aesthetic that honors the past while embracing the future. This careful orchestration of old and new elements fosters a sense of continuity and identity, which is often lost in cities experiencing rapid modernization.

In economic development, historic preservation has proven to be a significant catalyst. By revitalizing historic districts and landmarks, cities can create vibrant, attractive centers of activity that draw tourists and residents alike. These areas often become hotspots for investment, with businesses eager to capitalize on the unique ambiance that historic settings provide. Moreover, preserved historic sites offer an irreplaceable authenticity that new constructions can rarely match, making them ideal locations for boutique shops, restaurants, and cultural venues that contribute to the city's economic dynamism.

Preserved historic buildings add immeasurable value to urban environments, enhancing the quality of life for city dwellers. These structures provide a visual and tactile connection to the past, enriching the urban experience and giving cities a unique character that new buildings alone cannot provide. Furthermore, preserving these sites often leads to the creation of public spaces that offer respite and recreation amidst the urban hustle. Parks, squares, and pedestrian-friendly streets that respect historical layouts improve urban livability by providing accessible, human-scaled environments conducive to social interaction and community activities.

Case Studies: Successful Integration in Urban Planning

The city of Savannah, Georgia, serves as an exemplary model of integrating historic preservation within modern urban development. The city's innovative zoning ordinances have facilitated the protection of its historic districts while allowing for careful modern development around these areas. The result is a vibrant city where modern office buildings and historic homes coexist, contributing to a dynamic economy and high quality of urban life. The emphasis on maintaining tree-lined streets and public squares, as established in the original city plan from the 18th century, continues to make Savannah a model for combining historical preservation with modern urban needs.

Similarly, the Pearl District in Portland, Oregon, demonstrates how a run-down industrial area can be transformed into one of the most desirable neighborhoods in the United States through thoughtful preservation and redevelopment. The district's revitalization plan included the preservation of historic railway buildings and warehouses, repurposed into apartments, shops, and art galleries. Integrating modern architecture and public green spaces alongside these historic structures has created a neighborhood that is both economically thriving and rich in character.

These case studies highlight the potential for historic preservation to enhance rather than hinder modern urban development. By viewing historic sites as assets rather than obstacles, cities can create enriched, livable environments that respect the past while accommodating the future.

As this chapter closes, the narrative woven through its sections underscores the profound connection between preservation and contemporary urban development. The strategies and examples discussed illuminate the practical pathways to achieving this harmony and celebrate the more profound value that preserved history brings to modern cityscapes. The insights garnered here will segue into exploring innovative funding strategies in the next chapter, which are crucial in supporting the sustainable integration of historic preservation in urban development. The journey through preservation continues to reveal its indispensable role in shaping not just the physical but also our cities' economic and social fabric.

Chapter 14: Ensuring Inclusivity and Ethical Revitalization

As cities and communities stand on the brink of transformation through revitalization efforts, the specter of displacement and gentrification looms, threatening to overshadow renewal benefits. This chapter delves into the complexities of revitalization, focusing on strategies that safeguard against the involuntary displacement of residents and the cultural dilution often seen in gentrifying neighborhoods. Understanding the full spectrum of impacts, engaging deeply with the community, and implementing thoughtful policies are pivotal in steering revitalization toward inclusivity and ethical practices. Here, you will find a blend of theoretical frameworks and real-world success stories that illustrate the potential for revitalization efforts to foster physical renewal, social equity, and community cohesion.

14.1 Strategies for Avoiding Displacement and Gentrification

Understanding Impacts

Revitalization projects, while bringing much-needed infrastructure improvements and economic opportunities, can inadvertently lead to displacement and gentrification if not carefully managed. Displacement occurs when current residents, often in economically disadvantaged or marginalized communities, are forced to move due to rising housing costs or redevelopment. Gentrification, a complex process where the character and demographics of a neighborhood change, typically follows an influx of more affluent residents, escalating property values, and a shift in the neighborhood's cultural fabric. Both phenomena can fracture communities, dilute local cultures, and create economic and social divides.

To mitigate these risks, it is crucial to approach revitalization with a clear understanding of these dynamics. Comprehensive impact assessments should be conducted prior to launching any project, evaluating potential economic pressures and demographic shifts that could lead to displacement. These assessments should consider not only the immediate effects of physical redevelopment but also longer-term socio-economic impacts, ensuring that the benefits of revitalization are equi- tably distributed among all community members.

Community Engagement

The cornerstone of any successful and ethical revitalization project is genuine, sustained community engagement. Engaging with residents, local businesses, and stakeholders fosters transparency and empowers communities to have a say in the projects that affect their lives. Effective engagement involves regular, open dialogues, participatory decision-making processes, and mechanisms for residents to express concerns and provide input. This inclusive approach ensures that revitalization projects reflect the needs and desires of the community, particularly those of historically marginalized groups.

To facilitate meaningful engagement, revitalization initiatives should employ a variety of communication methods tailored to the community's needs, including public meetings, workshops, social media, and direct outreach. Engagement should be viewed as an ongoing process, not a one-time requirement. Continuous interaction helps build trust, ensures community members are informed of developments, and allows project planners to adjust plans in response to community feedback.

Policy Recommendations

To prevent displacement and manage gentrification, specific policies and strategies must be implemented. Inclusionary zoning, for example, is a policy tool that requires a certain percentage of new housing to be affordable for low-to-moderate-income households. This type of zoning ensures that revitalization includes housing options accessible to existing residents, helping to maintain the socio-economic diversity of neighborhoods.

Community land trusts (CLTs) offer another effective strategy. CLTs are non-profit, community-based organizations designed to ensure community stewardship of land. By acquiring and managing land for the benefit of the community, CLTs can provide affordable housing and prevent market forces from causing displacement. Additionally, policies that protect tenants from abrupt evictions and rent hikes are critical in stabilizing neighborhoods during periods of change.

Success Stories

Examining neighborhoods that have undergone revitalization without displacing residents provides valuable lessons and affirmations that ethical revitalization is achievable. One notable example is the Dudley Street Neighborhood Initiative in Boston, Massachusetts. This initiative, driven by a diverse coalition of residents, successfully revitalized the area through a community land trust that prevented displacement and encouraged local development without gentrification.

Another example is found in Portland, Oregon, where the city implemented a Right to Return policy for historically displaced populations. This policy prioritizes these individuals and families in new affordable housing developments in their former neighborhoods, acknowledging past injustices and actively working to rectify them. Such policies help maintain neighborhoods' cultural and social fabric and promote a sense of justice and reconciliation.

These success stories share common threads of robust community involvement, proactive policy measures, and a com- mitment to social equity. They serve as beacons, guiding other cities and communities in balancing revitalization with ethical responsibility and inclusivity.

14.2 Inclusive Community Planning: Ensuring Voices Are Heard

In the fabric of community planning, every thread counts, especially those that are often overlooked. The goal of inclusive community planning is not merely to decorate the planning process with a veneer of diversity but to weave the rich, varied experiences and insights of all community members into the very heart of revitalization efforts. Ensuring diverse community representation means more than just having a seat at the table—it involves actively engaging and amplifying the voices of marginalized and historically underrepresented groups. This commitment transforms the planning landscape to reflect a tapestry that is vivid with the colors of all its constituents.

A primary challenge in achieving this is the historical inertia of exclusionary practices that have sidelined certain groups based on race, economic status, or cultural background. To counteract this, it is crucial to proactively identify and involve these groups from the outset of planning. This might include partnering with local organizations that work directly with these communities or setting up advisory panels that include representatives from these groups to ensure their perspectives are integrated into decision-making processes. For instance, in areas where Indigenous communities reside, it is vital to respect and incorporate their ancestral knowledge and land rights into urban planning, which not only preserves their heritage but also enriches the cultural and environmental stewardship of the project.

Facilitating meaningful participation extends beyond physical presence. It encompasses creating environments where all participants feel genuinely welcomed and valued for their contributions. This involves logistical considerations like organizing meetings at times that are convenient for working individuals or providing childcare to increase accessibility for parents. Language translation services and the availability of materials in multiple formats (audio, visual, printed, digital) ensure that language barriers do not impede participation. Moreover, the advent of digital tools and platforms can significantly enhance inclusivity, allowing people who cannot attend in person to contribute their views. Virtual town halls, interactive surveys, and digital forums can be particularly effective in engaging younger demographics and those who are tech-savvy, ensuring a broader spectrum of community input.

The value of local knowledge must be balanced in shaping

projects that resonate with community needs and aspirations. Residents often hold a deep understanding of their neighborhood's history, challenges, and subtle nuances that might not be apparent to external planners. This local expertise can significantly enhance the relevance and effectiveness of revitalization projects. For example, in planning a new public park, input from local residents can inform not only the design but also essential features that cater to local needs, such as safe, inclusive play areas for children, walking paths for seniors, and community gardens that reflect the community's agricultural heritage. By valuing and integrating this local knowledge, plan- ners can develop functional and deeply meaningful solutions for the community.

Monitoring the inclusivity of the planning process is as crucial as the initial engagement. This ongoing evaluation ensures the process remains open, transparent, and responsive to all community input, adapting as necessary to address any emerging issues or feedback. Effective monitoring can be facilitated by establishing clear benchmarks for inclusivity at the outset and regularly assessing progress against these benchmarks. Tools such as feedback forms, community satisfaction surveys, and independent audits can provide valuable insights into how inclusive the process is and highlight areas for improvement. Regular reports on these evaluations should be made public to maintain transparency and build trust among community members, reinforcing their confidence in the process and its commitment to inclusivity.

Inclusive community planning is about crafting spaces and places that reflect and celebrate the community's diversity.

It involves a deliberate and thoughtful approach that seeks to understand and integrate the unique tapestry of community voices into the planning and development of physically inclusive spaces and socially and culturally vibrant spaces. By committing to these principles, planners, and developers can ensure that revitalization projects are about building environments and fostering community well-being and cohesion.

14.3 Affordable Housing Solutions Within Historic Districts

Integrating affordable housing into historic districts presents a unique challenge: How do we preserve our communities' invaluable architectural heritage while simultaneously address- ing the pressing need for affordable living spaces? This delicate balance requires innovative strategies that respect the past yet embrace the future. As urban populations grow and the demand for accessible housing increases, historic districts must evolve, adopting inclusive approaches that do not compromise their character or integrity.

One effective strategy for integrating affordable housing within these areas involves the adaptive reuse of historic buildings. By converting underutilized historic structures—such as old schools, factories, or warehouses—into housing, we preserve the architectural integrity while providing new utility. This ap- proach prevents the decay and potential demolition of historic sites and revitalizes them as living spaces that contribute to the community's socio-economic diversity. However, for adaptive reuse to be successful, careful consideration must be given to the design process. It is essential to maintain the historical elements that define the building's character while retrofitting them with modern amenities and ensuring compliance with current building codes and accessibility standards.

Policy tools and incentives play a pivotal role in encouraging affordable housing development in historic districts. Tax credits, such as the Federal Historic Preservation Tax Incentives program, offer financial benefits to developers who restore and adapt historic buildings for affordable housing purposes. These incentives make projects financially viable and attract investment into areas that might otherwise be overlooked. Additionally, density bonuses can be a compelling tool. Municipalities might offer developers the opportunity to increase the density of their projects—allowing more housing units than normally permitted—provided they include a certain percentage of affordable housing units or agree to preserve significant historical features.

Showcasing successful examples provides tangible insights into the practical application of these strategies. Consider the transformation of the Baker Chocolate Factory in Massachusetts. This historic complex was converted into a mixed-income housing development, with a portion of its units designated as affordable. The project preserved the factory's distinctive architectural features, including its red brick exterior and large windows, while providing vital housing to the community. Another example is found in the heart of San Francisco, where the Richardson Apartments were developed. This project provided affordable housing and included on-site social services, demonstrating a holistic approach to community development in historic settings.

Best practices for balancing the goals of historic preservation with the need for affordable housing emphasize the importance of community involvement and comprehensive planning. Engaging with local residents, historians, and urban planners from the outset can help identify the most cherished historical features and how they can be preserved or incorporated into new developments. Planning should be iterative, allowing feedback and adjustments that refine the project's scope and design to meet community needs and preservation standards better. Moreover, employing environmentally sustainable practices in these projects can further enhance their value, making them affordable, historical, and green.

As we navigate the complexities of revitalizing our historic districts, the integration of affordable housing is crucial in ensuring these areas remain vibrant and inclusive. We can foster rich communities in history and opportunity through thoughtful planning, innovative policies, and a commitment to preserving the past while accommodating present needs.

In wrapping up this exploration of affordable housing solutions within historic districts, we've traversed from the synergies of adaptive reuse to the practicalities of policy incentives, illuminated by real-world examples demonstrating the potential for historic districts to evolve inclusively. As we turn the page, we anticipate further discussions on innovative funding strategies that support these vital integration efforts, ensuring the sustainability of our cherished historic environments in the chapters to come.

Chapter 15: Measuring Success and Sustaining Momentum

As you step into the realm of town and historic revitalization, understanding how to gauge the impact of your efforts becomes paramount. This chapter, "Measuring Success and Sustaining Momentum," is designed to equip you with the tools needed to not only assess the effectiveness of your projects but to also use these insights to refine and enhance future endeavors. Imagine you are not just building or renovating structures but weaving a vibrant tapestry of community, history, and sustainability. The way you measure success should reflect this multifaceted approach, capturing the economic, social, and environmental outcomes that genuinely define the transformative power of revitalization.

15.1 Metrics for Success: Assessing Economic, Social, and Environmental Outcomes

Defining Success

Success in revitalization projects isn't just about the finished aesthetic appeal or the preservation of historical accuracy, as important as these are. It extends to the economic upliftment, social cohesion, and environmental sustainability that these projects foster. Establishing clear metrics for each of these outcomes is crucial. Economic impact can be quantified in terms of job creation, increased property values, and tourism revenues. Social cohesion can be assessed by the extent of community involvement and the improvement in the quality of life for residents. Environmental sustainability measures might include reducing carbon emissions, increasing green spaces, and promoting sustainable local businesses. Each metric provides a lens through which the broader implications of a revitalization project can be evaluated, giving you a comprehensive view of its benefits.

Data Collection and Analysis

Collecting robust data is the backbone of effective project assessment. For economic impacts, sources such as local business revenue reports, property value assessments, and employment rates are invaluable. Social outcomes can be gauged through surveys that explore community satisfaction and participation rates. Environmental metrics often require data on energy consumption, waste management, and biodiversity indices. Analyzing this data provides a factual basis to evaluate the success of your revitalization efforts. This process highlights achievements and pinpoints areas needing improvement, guiding strategic adjustments.

Adjusting Strategies

The dynamic nature of revitalization work means strategies must evolve based on ongoing data analysis. If employment has not increased as anticipated, the project may need a stronger focus on creating job opportunities through local vendor preferences or skills training programs. If community feedback indicates a desire for more green spaces, subsequent phases of the project can adjust to include these preferences. This adaptive approach ensures that revitalization efforts remain aligned with community needs and environmental goals, increasing their overall effectiveness and sustainability.

Reporting and Transparency

Openness in sharing successes and lessons learned with stakeholders is fundamental to the trust-building process. Regular, transparent reporting using clear, accessible formats helps demystify the data and allows stakeholders to see both the impacts of their contributions and areas where further support isneeded. These reports should celebrate milestones and articulate challenges without glossing over them. Engaging visuals like infographics can help illustrate successes and ongoing efforts effectively, making the information relatable and easy to understand for everyone, irrespective of their familiarity with the project details.

Interactive Element: Reflective Journaling Prompt

To deepen your understanding and personal connection to the revitalization efforts, take a moment to reflect on the following prompt: "Consider a revitalization project you are familiar with or involved in. Based on what you've learned about defining success, what specific economic, social, and environmental metrics could effectively measure its impact? How could this data be collected, and what strategies might be adjusted based on this analysis?" This exercise not only reinforces the concepts discussed but also encourages a personal stake in applying these strategies, fostering a deeper engagement with the revitalization process.

15.2 Building a Legacy: Long-Term Preservation Strategies

In the realm of town and historic revitalization, the fruits of your labor are not just seen in the immediate enhancements and restorations but truly manifest in their ability to stand the test of time. As someone deeply involved in these efforts, you understand that the sustainability of preservation is an ongoing commitment that extends far beyond the ribbon-cutting ceremony. It involves a meticulous blend of maintenance, funding, community support, and forward-looking planning to ensure these treasured sites continue to enrich lives for generations to come.

Sustainability in preservation is multifaceted, encompassing the physical upkeep of structures, the financial mechanisms that support such activities, and the community engagement that breathes life into these endeavors. Maintenance, often overlooked in the excitement of project completion, is critical. It requires a strategic approach where preservation experts, local artisans, and conservationists collaborate to address the natural wear and tear that historic sites endure. Techniques and materials used in maintenance must be carefully chosen to respect the site's historical integrity while employing modern advancements for durability and environmental sustainability. Funding these activities is equally crucial, relying on a mix of public grants, private donations, and innovative funding models like endowments or heritage trusts that ensure a steady flow of resources dedicated to ongoing upkeep.

Planning for the legacy of revitalization projects, known as legacy planning, is about embedding the future into the present efforts. This strategic foresight involves not only preserving the physical structure but also maintaining its relevance to future generations. It's about creating a narrative that connects the past with the future, making these sites perennial sources of cultural pride and historical education. For instance, integrating technology like augmented reality can offer future visitors new ways to experience historical sites, thus keeping the engagement contemporary and dynamic. Legacy planning also considers the environmental impact of preservation, advocating for green practices that ensure the site's sustainability aligns with global efforts to combat climate change.

Stewardship programs represent a proactive approach to preservation, where community members, local businesses, and governmental bodies share the caretaking responsibility. These programs often involve training locals in preservation techniques, fostering a sense of ownership and connection to the site. Partnerships with educational institutions can facilitate this, integrating preservation into the curriculum and encouraging a hands-on approach to learning. Furthermore, stewardship can extend to partnerships with corporate entities that seek to contribute to community efforts guided by well-structured corporate social responsibility initiatives. These collaborations can provide the necessary financial and volunteer support critical to the long-term maintenance and success of preservation projects.

Continual community engagement and education are the lifeblood of sustainable preservation. It's one thing to restore a building and another to keep the community invested in its future. Ongoing educational programs that highlight the site's historical significance and its role in the community can keep public interest alive. These programs might include workshops, guided tours, and interactive seminars that delve into the site's past and its current and future role in the community. Engaging the community through events allows for the reiteration of the site's value and encourages the public to take active roles in its preservation. By fostering a knowledgeable and concerned community, you ensure that today's efforts will be appreciated and continued by the stewards of tomorrow.

Each aspect of building a legacy in historic preservation underscores a commitment not just to the past but to the future. It requires a thoughtful blend of respecting historical integrity, leveraging modern technology and practices, and cultivating a community deeply connected to its heritage. This approach ensures that the stories and significance of our historical sites are not lost but are instead passed down, rich and intact, to the generations that follow.

15.3 Celebrating Success: Fostering Pride and Ownership in Revitalized Communities

Revitalization projects, by their very nature, are monumental undertakings that reshape the physical landscape and, perhaps more importantly, rejuvenate the spirit and pride of a community. Recognizing and celebrating these achievements plays a pivotal role in embedding a lasting sense of accomplishment and ownership among those who live and work within these transformed environments. Imagine unveiling a restored his- toric landmark where the local community gathers to celebrate the culmination of hard work and shared visions. Such events are not just parties; they are crucial for knitting the fabric of the community tighter together, instilling a collective pride in their shared heritage and renewed space.

Recognition and Celebration

Effective recognition goes beyond mere acknowledgment; it involves creating memorable, engaging events that highlight the community's role in the revitalization process. Organizing award ceremonies that honor local businesses and individuals who have contributed significantly to the project rewards effort and stimulates ongoing community involvement and investment. Public acknowledgments, whether through plaques, press releases, or mentions in local media, serve to embed the project into the community's collective memory. Additionally, community events like festivals or markets, ideally held in the revitalized spaces, not only celebrate the completion of the project but also demonstrate the functional enhancements brought by the revitalization. These festivities should be inclusive, reflecting the community's cultural diversity, and featuring local artists, creators, and performers, strengthening local cultural identity and economic vitality.

Building Community Pride

The transformation of a physical space can have a profound impact on community pride. When you see your efforts materialize in the form of a beautifully revitalized town square or a bustling market street, it reinforces a sense of ownership and pride in the enhancements to your community. This emotional investment is crucial for the sustained success of revitalization efforts. It transforms public spaces into 'our spaces,' where each element, from benches and lamps to walkways and signage, tells a story of collective effort and shared history. Engaging the community from the outset is essential to cultivating this sentiment, ensuring that the project reflects their needs and aspirations and keeping them informed and involved throughout the process. When the community sees their input visibly shaping their environment, it strengthens their connection to the place and to each other, fostering a resilient community fabric that can withstand the ebbs and flows of social and economic changes.

Sharing Success Stories

Communicating the successes of revitalization projects can inspire other communities and promote a broader understanding of the value of historic preservation. Utilizing various media outlets to share stories and outcomes not only garners recognition for the community's efforts but also serves as a beacon for similar initiatives elsewhere. These narratives highlight the challenges overcome and the strategies employed, providing a realistic yet optimistic roadmap for others. Furthermore, showcasing these stories in community newsletters, local broadcasts, and social media platforms ensures that the success is celebrated widely and that the community receives due recognition for their hard work and innovative ideas. This bolsters local morale and attracts visitors and investors, contributing to a cycle of ongoing improvement and revitalization.

Engaging Youth

The inclusion of the younger generation in these celebrations and educational programs is not merely beneficial; it is essential for the long-term sustainability of preservation efforts. Young people can form a personal connection with their town's heritage and ongoing development by involving schools, youth clubs, and educational organizations in celebration events, whether through guided tours, interactive workshops, or creative competitions. This engagement helps to instill a sense of responsibility and pride in maintaining and respecting these revitalized spaces. Furthermore, incorporating modern technology and social media into these educational activities can significantly enhance their appeal, making them more accessible and engaging for a digital-savvy generation. This educates them about their heritage and the importance of community involvement and empowers them to be active participants in future preservation and revitalization efforts.

Through these celebrations and engagements, revitalization projects do more than just restore buildings or streets—they rejuvenate the community's spirit, strengthen its pride, and ensure its legacy continues to inspire the current residents and generations to come.

15.4 Leveraging Success for Future Projects: A Scalable Model

The success of a revitalization project is not just a capstone; it's a stepping stone. Each successful project provides a blueprint, a set of strategies that worked, which can be adapted and scaled for future initiatives. This scalability ensures that the lessons learned are not siloed but serve as a springboard for broader applications, helping other communities and projects benefit from proven successes. This subchapter explores how the achievements of individual projects can be leveraged to create scalable models that enhance the efficacy and reach of future revitalization efforts.

Scalable Models

Creating scalable models from successful revitalization projects involves distilling the core components that contribute to their success. These components often include effective project management techniques, innovative funding solutions, community engagement strategies, and sustainability practices. By identifying these essential elements, you can develop a framework that can be tailored to suit different contexts without reinventing the wheel each time. For example, suppose a particular approach to integrating green technology in a historic district proved effective. This approach can be templated and adapted to other districts, adjusting for local nuances such as climate, available technologies, and community preferences. This not only saves time and resources but also builds on a foundation of proven success, reducing risk for future projects.

Knowledge Transfer

The transfer of knowledge is critical in ensuring that the insights gained from successful projects propagate effectively. This can be achieved through various channels, such as detailed case studies, workshops, publications, and mentor- ship programs. Workshops and seminars that bring together professionals from different regions provide a platform for sharing experiences and strategies. These interactions foster a collaborative learning environment where practical knowledge is exchanged, from handling regulatory challenges to engaging diverse community groups. Publications that document the successes and lessons of projects serve as valuable resources for those planning similar endeavors. Furthermore, establishing mentorship programs where seasoned professionals guide new teams can help transfer tacit knowledge and nuanced understandings that are often lost in written reports.

Building Partnerships

The importance of building strategic partnerships cannot be overstated. Collaborations with other communities, non-profit organizations, government entities, and private sectors can significantly amplify the impact of revitalization efforts. These partnerships can provide a multitude of resources, from funding to expertise, and can help navigate bureaucratic processes more smoothly. For instance, partnering with environmental organizations can provide access to sustainability experts who can advise on the best practices for incorporating eco-friendly technologies and methods into revitalization projects. Similarly, collaborations with academic institutions can facilitate research studies that assess the impact of revitalization efforts, providing data that can strengthen grant applications and policy proposals.

Funding and Resources

Securing funding and resources for future projects based on the success of completed efforts involves showcasing the tangible benefits of past projects. This can be accomplished through impact reports highlighting cultural and historical improvements and economic benefits such as job creation and increased tourism. These reports make a compelling case to potential funders about the return on investment offered by revitalization projects. Additionally, successful projects can attract funding through awards and recognition from preservation and urban development communities, which often come with financial grants. Crowdfunding platforms present another avenue to capitalize on the public visibility and community goodwill generated by successful projects, turning public support into financial backing.

By focusing on these areas, the knowledge and success of individual revitalization projects can be transformed into scalable models that benefit wider regions and future generations. This approach maximizes the impact of successful initiatives and fosters a culture of continuous improvement and collective benefit in historic preservation and community revitalization.

15.5 The Role of Education in Sustaining Preservation Efforts

The ongoing success of any revitalization or historic preserva- tion effort significantly hinges on the level of public awareness and education about the importance of these initiatives. Developing comprehensive educational programs and resources plays a pivotal role in fostering a deep, sustained appreciation and understanding of the value of preserving our historical heritage. Such educational endeavors disseminate crucial information and inspire community members to actively participate in preservation activities. They transform historical awareness from a passive acknowledgment into an active, engaged practice that benefits the entire community.

Educational programs tailored to historic preservation can take various forms, each designed to cater to different segments of the community. For schoolchildren, curricula can be developed that integrate local history and architecture into subjects like social studies, art, and science. For adults, continuing education courses offered through local colleges or community centers can delve into more complex aspects of preservation, such as the techniques used in restoring historical buildings or the economic benefits of maintaining historical sites within a community. These programs should aim not merely to inform but to captivate, utilizing the rich narratives of the past to enrich the educational experience. To facilitate this, partnerships with local museums, historical societies, and preservation experts can provide authentic insights and opportunities for experiential learning, such as guided tours of historical sites or hands-on workshops in traditional building techniques.

Furthermore, the collaboration between schools and community organizations offers a robust framework for promoting preservation education. Schools can serve as vital conduits for information dissemination, reaching families and community members who might not otherwise engage with preservation efforts. With their deep local connections and understanding, community organizations can provide the real-world applications and relevance of these educational initiatives, making the area's history tangible and pertinent. For example, a community organization could coordinate with schools to host an annual heritage day, where students present projects on local history and creators and craftspeople demonstrate traditional skills. Such events not only educate but also celebrate the community's unique cultural heritage, reinforcing the importance of preservation efforts.

In today's digital age, the use of online resources and platforms significantly enhances the reach and effectiveness of educational programs. Developing a dedicated website or digital platform that offers educational materials, interactive learning modules, videos, and virtual tours can make preservation education accessible to a broader audience. These platforms can serve as information archives, continuously updated with the latest research, project updates, and educational materials. They can also facilitate interactive experiences, such as webinars with preservation experts or online forums where community members can discuss local history and preservation issues. This digital approach extends the geographical reach of educational efforts. It caters to the modern populace's preference for digital consumption, ensuring that the messages of preservation are received and retained by a broader, more technologically savvy audience.

Organizing public workshops and seminars is another effective method to engage the community and provide education on historic preservation. These events can be tailored to address specific aspects of preservation, such as the economic impact of historic districts, the environmental benefits of using traditional materials, or the process of securing a property on the National Register of Historic Places. Featuring experts, practitioners, and community leaders as speakers can lend credibility and depth to the discussions, drawing larger audiences. These gatherings serve as educational opportunities and forums for community members to voice concerns, ask questions, and directly engage with experts, fostering a more informed and involved community base. These seminars and workshops enhance transparency in preservation efforts and encourage greater community participation by providing a platform for open dialogue.

15.6 Next Steps: Expanding the Scope of Revitalization Efforts

As you delve deeper into the world of town and historic revitalization, it becomes increasingly evident that strategic planning is not merely a preliminary step but a continuous process that adapts and evolves with each phase of development. The importance of strategic planning lies in its ability to anticipate future needs and challenges while identifying new opportunities for growth and improvement. As you consider expanding the scope of your revitalization efforts, it is crucial to maintain a forward-thinking approach, one that encompasses not only the immediate needs of the community but also its long-term aspirations. This involves a thorough analysis of demographic trends, economic conditions, and cultural shifts, which can provide valuable insights into how a town or historic area might evolve in the coming years.

Exploring innovative approaches to preservation and revitalization is crucial as it injects new life into traditional practices. Embracing technology, for instance, can transform conventional methods of restoration and maintenance. Imagine integrating augmented reality to offer immersive historical tours or using advanced materials that offer better durability and environmental sustainability without compromising the aesthetic integrity of historic structures. Moreover, interdisciplinary collaboration expands the horizons of what can be achieved in revitalization projects. By bringing together experts from fields such as urban planning, architecture, environmental science, and even sociology, you can develop more comprehensive and inclusive strategies that address various factors affecting revitalization projects.

Community visioning plays a pivotal role in aligning revitalization efforts with the community's aspirations. This process involves engaging community members in discussions and workshops where they can express their hopes, concerns, and visions for the future of their town or neighborhood. It is a dynamic process that not only fosters a deeper connection between residents and the revitalization projects but also ensures that these initiatives reflect the true spirit and needs of the community. Through community visioning, residents become co-creators of their environment, actively participating in shaping the development that affects their lives. This collaborative approach helps build a sense of ownership and pride among community members, which is essential for revitalization efforts' long-term success and sustainability.

Speaking of sustainability, ensuring the sustainable growth of revitalization projects is paramount. This means finding a balance between development and preservation, economic growth and environmental protection, modernity and heritage. Sustainable growth strategies include implementing green building practices, promoting local businesses and crafts, and preserving natural landscapes and ecosystems within and around historic sites. Moreover, sustainability involves creating economic opportunities that do not exploit but instead enhance the cultural and historical assets of the community. By prioritizing sustainability, you ensure that revitalization efforts contribute to the well-being of both the environment and the community, creating a legacy of mindful development that respects and preserves the past while looking forward to the future.

Navigating through these next steps in expanding the scope of revitalization efforts, you are invited to reflect on the broader implications of your work. It's about more than just restoring buildings or beautifying streets—it's about reknitting the social fabric, reinvigorating community pride, and responsibly stewarding cultural and historical treasures into the future. As this chapter closes, remember that each step taken in strategic planning, innovative approach adoption, community visioning, and promoting sustainable growth redefines the physical landscape and reshapes the community's identity and trajectory toward a prosperous, inclusive future. As you move forward, carry with you the lessons learned and the successes achieved, ready to apply them to new challenges and opportunities that await in the continuing saga of revitalization.

Conclusion

As we draw the curtains on our exploration of town and historic revitalization, we must reflect on the profound impact such endeavors can have on our communities. Throughout this book, we've explored the importance of revitalizing our towns and historic sites, not merely as acts of preservation but as vital undertakings that rejuvenate our cultural identity, enhance community cohesion, stimulate economic growth, and contribute to environmental sustainability.

We've navigated through many strategies and solutions essential for initiating, planning, and executing successful revitalization projects. From engaging the community to securing funding, overcoming regulatory challenges, and blending modern amenities with historical integrity—each step is a building block toward transforming our urban landscapes while honoring their historical significance.

The role of community involvement cannot be overstated. It is the backbone of successful revitalization efforts, embodying the spirit of collective action. This book has emphasized the power of community engagement as a catalyst for meaningful change, urging each of you to take an active role in the preser- vation and enhancement of your locales.

I encourage you to apply these insights to your towns and historic sites. Become advocates, volunteers, or leaders in your local preservation efforts. Your proactive participation can ignite the spark needed to revitalize and transform your community into a vibrant hub that respects its past while looking confidently toward the future.

Reflecting on the journey of writing this book, I am filled with hope. Hope for the countless towns and historic sites that stand on the brink of decay and neglect, and hope for our ability to bring them back to life. Together, we can ensure that these places not only survive but thrive, preserving their stories and heritage while adapting to the needs of modern life.

I wish to acknowledge the tireless efforts of everyone involved in town and historic revitalization—from local activists and community members to professionals in urban planning, architecture, and preservation. Your dedication and hard work are the linchpins of success in these projects.

I invite you to share your stories and experiences with revitalization. Connect with me through social media, email, or community forums. Your insights and successes enrich our collective knowledge and inspire others to embark on similar journeys.

For those eager to dive deeper, a list of additional resources is provided at the end of this book. These websites, organizations, and reading materials are tools for further exploration and empowerment in your revitalization endeavors.

Let us part with an uplifting message: revitalization is not just about restoring buildings but about rekindling the spirits of our communities. It's about creating spaces where past and future merge, crafting environments where every generation can thrive. Together, let's continue to breathe new life into our streets and structures, forging a path that respects our heritage and embraces our future.

Together, we build tomorrow.

Resources

Websites

National Trust for Historic Preservation - savingplaces.org
- Offers resources and grants for preserving historic places.

The Association for Preservation Technology International (APT) - apti.org
- Provides technical resources for preservation professioals.

Preservation Directory - preservationdirectory.com
- Directory of historic preservation resources and organizations.

National Park Service (NPS) - Preservation - nps.gov
· Offers guidelines, grants, and technical preservation services.

American Planning Association (APA) - Historic Preservation - planning.org
· Resources and best practices for planners involved in preservation.

Organizations

National Trust for Historic Preservation - savingplaces.org
· Leading nonprofit organization dedicated to historic preservation in the U.S.

Historic New England - historicnewengland.org
· Non profit preserving and sharing New England's cultural heritage.

The National Main Street Center - mainstreet.org
· Focuses on revitalizing historic downtowns and neighborhood commercial districts.

The Association for Preservation Technology International (APT) - apti.org

- Dedicated to advancing appropriate traditional and new technologies to protect and preserve historic structures and sites.

Partners for Sacred Places - sacredplaces.org

- Supports the stewardship and active community use of historic sacred places.

Reading Materials (Books)

"A Richer Heritage: Historic Preservation in the Twenty-First Century" - Edited by Robert E. Stipe

- Comprehensive overview of the preservation movement in the U.S.

"Historic Preservation: An Introduction to Its History, Principles, and Practice" - Norman Tyler, Ted J. Ligibel, Ilene R. Tyler

- Introductory text covering the key aspects of historic preservation.

"New Solutions for House Museums: Ensuring the Long-Term Preservation of America's Historic Houses" - Donna Ann Harris

· Discusses strategies for maintaining historic house museums.

"Preserving the World's Great Cities: The Destruction and Renewal of the Historic Metropolis" - Anthony Tung

· Explores the preservation efforts in major cities around the world.

"Saving America's Treasures" - David Brown, Charles E. Fisher, John H. Sprinkle Jr.

· Provides case studies of successful preservation projects.

Government Resources

National Park Service (NPS) - Technical Preservation Services   - nps.gov

· Offers technical preservation resources and guidance.

State Historic Preservation Offices (SHPOs) - Varies by state
· State-specific resources and support for preservation projects.

Advisory Council on Historic Preservation (ACHP) - achp.gov
· Promotes the preservation, enhancement, and sustainable use of the nation's diverse historic resources.

Library of Congress - Historic American Buildings Survey (HABS) - loc.gov
· Documentation of historic buildings and sites.

U.S. Department of Housing and Urban Development (HUD) - Historic Preservation - hud.gov
· Programs and grants supporting preservation in urban areas.

Academic Resources

Columbia University GSAPP - Historic Preservation - arch.columbia.edu
· Academic program offering resources and research inhistoric preservation.

Goucher College - MA in Historic Preservation - goucher.edu

· Graduate program with resources for preservation professionals.

University of Florida - Historic Preservation Program - dcp.ufl.edu

· Offers various resources and research opportunities in historic preservation.

University of Massachusetts Amherst - Center for Heritage and Society - umass.edu

· Research center focusing on heritage and preservation studies.

Savannah College of Art and Design (SCAD) - Historic Preservation - scad.edu

· Provides academic resources and research opportunities in historic preservation.

References

• *Case Studies from Successful DRI Communities & Projects*
https://www.ny.gov/downtown-revitalization-initiative/dri-focus-case-studies-successful-dri-communities-p rojects

• *National Park Service Historic Preservation Economic Impact*
https://www.nps.gov/subjects/historicpreservation/economic-impacts.htm

• *Why Connected Neighborhoods Are Key to Urban Revitalization*
https://www.gensler.com/blog/why-connected-neighborhoods-are-key-to-urban-revitalization

• *Comparing Environmental Impact of Building New Hometown*
https://www.renewableenergymagazine.com/rose-mor
rison/comparing-environmental-impact-of-building-new-home-
20230314#:~:text=Generally%2C%20renovatin
g%20an%20existing%20building,air%2C%20water%20a
nd%20noise%20pollution

• *Financial Feasibility Analysis for Your Revitalization …*
https://ced.sog.unc.edu/2019/06/local-governments-
financial-feasibility-analysis-for-your-revitalization-pr ojects/

• *Case Studies from Successful DRI Communities & Projects*
https://www.ny.gov/downtown-revitalization-initiative/dri-focus-
case-studies-successful-dri-communities-projects

• *What is Community Engagement and Why is It Crucial for Urban Planning*
https://www.allthingsurban.net/blog/What-is-Community-
Engagement-and-Why-is-It-Crucial-for-Urban-Planning

• *Historic Preservationists: What They Are and What They Do*
https://www.indeed.com/career-advice/finding-a-job/wh at-is-
historic-preservationist

REFERENCES

• *Historic Preservation Fund Competitive Grant Sample ...*
https://www.nps.gov/articles/000/historic-preservation-fund-
sample-grant-applications.htm

• *New Year, New Building: 5 Adaptive Reuse Projects...*https://s
avingplaces.org/stories/new-year-new-building-6-adaptive-reuse-
projects-for-historic-buildings

• *Beyond Gentrification: Strategies for Guiding the Conversation*
https://www.jchs.harvard.edu/sites/default/files/w14-1 2_brown.pdf

• *Community Benefits Agreements: A New Local ...* https://fur
mancenter.org/files/publications/Community_Benefits_
Agreements_Working_Paper.pdf

•*Historic Preservation Tax Incentives*
https://www.nps.gov/subjects/taxincentives/

• *Catalyzing Change: The Role of Public-Private Partnerships in…*
https://medium.com/@Ecotone_PBC/catalyzing-change-the-role-
of-public-private-partnerships-in-impactful-urban-renewal-
67a9624de96f

• *New Crowdfunding Campaign to Restore Nina Simone's …*
https://savingplaces.org/places/ninasimone/updates/cro
wdfunding-campaign-for-nina-simone-home

• *Navigating Historic Tax Credits: How a Preservation …*
https://www.baileyedward.com/insights/navigating-historic-tax-
credits-how-a-preservation-architect-can-maximize-your-
investment/

• *A Guidebook to Community Engagement: Involving Urban and*
https://www.canr.msu.edu/uploads/375/65790/Guidebo
oktoCommunityEngagement_FINAL_Sept2014.pdf

• *How to Organize a Town Hall Meeting A Planning Guide*
https://guideinc.org/wp-content/uploads/2015/07/Organizing-a-
Town-Hall-Meeting.pdf

• *Online Community Engagement Tools - EngagementHQ*
https://granicus.com/blog/engagementhq-online-community-engagement-tools/

• *Case Studies from Successful DRI Communities & Projects*
https://www.ny.gov/downtown-revitalization-initiative/dri-focus-case-studies-successful-dri-communities-p rojects

• *New Year, New Building: 5 Adaptive Reuse Projects for HistoricBuildings https://savingplaces.org/stories/new-year-new-building-6-adaptive-reuse-projects-for-historic-buildin gs*

• *7 Grassroots Strategies Empowering Urban Communities*
https://www.planetizen.com/blogs/110506-7-grassroots-strategies-empowering-urban-communities

• *Historic Preservation Advocacy to Help Overcome the Housing Crisis*
https://savingplaces.org/stories/historic-preservation-advocacy-to-help-overcome-the-housing-crisis

• *Case Studies on the Conservation and Management of ...*
https://whc.unesco.org/en/activities/634/

• *Smart Building Technology in Historical Preservation*
https://green.org/2024/01/30/smart-building-technology-in-hist
orical-preservation/

• *Understanding ADA Requirements for Historic Properties*
https://www.globest.com/2019/09/17/understanding-ada-
requirements-for-historic-properties/

• *Case Studies on the Conservation and Management of ...*
https://whc.unesco.org/en/activities/634/

• *Technical Assistance - Historic Preservation Fund (U.S. ...*
https://www.nps.gov/subjects/historicpreservationfund/technical-
assistance.htm

• *Sustainable Historic Preservation*
https://www.wbdg.org/design-objectives/historic-
preservation/sustainable-historic-preservation

REFERENCES

• *Evaluating the Implementation of Energy Retrofits in …*
https://www.mdpi.com/2571-9408/7/2/48

• *Sustainable Historic Preservation*
https://www.wbdg.org/design-objectives/historic-
preservation/sustainable-historic-preservation

• *How six small towns and cities are going green*
https://archive.curbed.com/2017/10/31/16580810/sustainable-
small-town-solar-power

• *The Key Role of VR in Preserving Cultural Heritage*
https://amt-lab.org/blog/2022/4/motivating-usages-of-virtual-
reality-in-cultural-heritage

• *9 crowdfunding platforms for charities,community groups and
social entrepreneurs*
https://www.nesta.org.uk/blog/9-crowdfunding-platforms-for-
charities-community-groups- and-social-entrepreneurs/

• *Harnessing Predictive Analytics for Urban Development*
https://atcresearch.co/guest-blog/harnessing-predict ive-analytics-for-urban-development/

• *"CaseStudy: How VR is Transforming the Museum Experience"*
https://www.vv360.co.uk/2024/02/05/case-study-how-v r-is-transforming-the-museum-experience/

• *Increasing Residential Density in Historic Environments*
https://historicengland.org.uk/images-books/publica tions/increasing-residential-density-in-historic-environ ments/160718-increasing-residential-density-in-historic-environments-final-report/

• *Recommendation on the Historic Urban Landscape*
https://whc.unesco.org/en/hul/

• *Public Transportation's Impact on Rural and Small Towns*
https://www.apta.com/wp-content/uploads/Resources/re sources/reportsandpublications/Documents/APTA-Rural-Transit-2017.pdf

REFERENCES

• *analysis of contribution of vertical garden sto urban sustainability:*
the case study of Antalya city, Turkey
*https://www.researchgate.net/publication/271208817_ANALYSIS_*
*OF_CONTRIBUTION_OF_VERTICAL_GARDENS_TO_URBAN_*
S USTAINABILITY_THE_CASE_STUDY_OF_ANTALYA_CI
TY_TURKEY

• *Creative Uses for Downtown Buildings in Small Towns*
https://economicdevelopment.extension.wisc.edu/arti
cles/creative-uses-for-downtown-buildings-in-small-t owns/

• *Agricultural Conservation Easement Program*
https://www.nrcs.usda.gov/programs-initiatives/acep-agricultural-
conservation-easement-program

• *Evaluating the impact of broadband access and internet …*
https://www.ncbi.nlm.nih.gov/pmc/articles/PMC98368 30/

•*A Case for Rural Broadband*
https://www.usda.gov/sites/default/files/documents/case-for-rural-
broadband.pdf

• *AdaptationStrategies-NOAA Office for Coastal Management*
ttps://coast.noaa.gov/digitalcoast/topics/climate-adaptation.html

• *Great Waterfront Case Studies*
https://www.pps.org/article/issuewaterfronts

•*Best Practices of Underwater Cultural Heritage*
https://www.unesco.org/en/underwater-heritage/best-practices

• *Community Engagement's Vital Role in Building Resilience*
https://givingcompass.org/article/community-engagement-s-vital-role-in-building-resilience

• *National Park Service Historic Preservation Economic Impact*
https://www.nps.gov/subjects/historicpreservation/economic-impacts.htm

•*20 Creative Adaptive Reuse Projects*
https://www.archdaily.com/783283/20-creative-adaptive-reuse-projects

REFERENCES

•*Six Practical Reasons to Save Old Buildings*
https://savingplaces.org/stories/six-reasons-save-old-buildings

• *Historic Preservation and Urban Revitalization in the Twenty*
https://journals.sagepub.com/doi/10.1177/088541221351 0524

• *Community Revitalization Is Hard to Get Right. Here's How It*
https://insight.kellogg.northwestern.edu/article/community-
revitalization-neighborhood-transformation-sustainable-
development

• *Can Community Land Trusts Help Maintain Affordability in Gentrifying Urban Areas*
https://housingmatters.urban.org/research-summary/can-
community-land-trusts-help-maintain-affordability-gentrifying-
urban-areas

• *Inclusive Community Engagement: Executive Guide* https://w
ww.c40knowledgehub.org/s/article/Inclusive-Community-
Engagement-Executive-Guide?language=en_US

• *Using Historic Preservation to Promote Affordability and …*
https://www.huduser.gov/portal/pdredge/pdr-edge-featd-article-121923.html

• *National Park Service Historic Preservation Economic Impact*
https://www.nps.gov/subjects/historicpreservation/economic-impacts.htm

• *Community Engagement Around Historic Preservation*
https://www.cultural-strategies.com/community-engagement-around-historic-preservation

• *30 Inspiring Urban Renewal Projects*
https://www.socialworkdegreeguide.com/30-inspiring-urban-renewal-projects/

• *Sustainable Historic Preservation*
https://www.wbdg.org/design-objectives/historic-preservation/sustainable-historic-preservation

About the Author

Harlan G. Otis is a life-long learner and an enthusiast of new experiences. With a passion for exploring diverse intellectual pursuits, he writes on a variety of subjects including multi-language learning, healthcare, finance, and business strategies. Harlan's writing aims to inspire and educate readers, offering deep insights and practical advice drawn from his own con- tinuous journey of discovery and personal growth. His work reflects a commitment to expanding knowledge and fostering a deeper understanding of the world around us.

Also by Harlan G. Otis

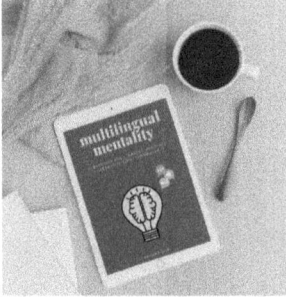

Multilingual Mentality:
Strategies for Learning Multiple
Languages Simultaneously

Introducing the essential guide
that will not only **accelerate** your
language acquisition but also
transform the way you view
learning languages forever.

'Multilingual Method: Strategies for Learning Multiple
Languages Simultaneously' is your passport to unlocking
the secrets behind fast, effective language learning.

www.ingramcontent.com/pod-product-compliance
Lightning Source LLC
Chambersburg PA
CBHW050458190326
41458CB00005B/1336